This Can't Be Tofu

DEBORAH MADISON

This
Can't
Be

TOFU

75 Recipes to Cook
Something You Never
Thought You Would—
and Love Every Bite

Ten Speed Press
Berkeley

Ten Speed Press and the Ten Speed Press colophon are registered trademarks of
Random House, Inc.

www.crownpublishing.com
www.tenspeed.com

Originally published in the United States by Clarkson Potter, New York, in 2000.

Library of Congress Cataloging-in-Publication Data
Madison, Deborah.
This can't be tofu! : 75 Recipes to Cook Something You Never Thought You Would—
and Love Every Bite / Deborah Madison—1st ed.
    p.   cm.
Includes index.
1. Cookery (Tofu)   I. Title.
TX814.5.T63 M34   2000
641.6'5655—dc21
                                99-040281
ISBN 978-0-7679-0419-3

Book design by Pei Loi Koay
Illustrations by Patrick McFarlin

20   19   18   17   16   15   14   13

First Edition

Acknowledgments

MY THANKS AND APPRECIATION go to all those who encouraged, aided and abetted in *This Can't Be Tofu!*, in particular, my favorite tofu eater, Patrick McFarlin, who kept saying, "This can't be tofu!" and thus named the book; Anne Marie Bough who cheerfully added recipe testing to her already demanding job as a line cook; Mark Mattern of Disney World, whose enthusiasm got me to enjoy my first of many tofu smoothies; Cheryl Jamison, who shared her considerable knowledge of smoke and spice, resulting in barbecued tofu; Harriet Bell, editor par excellence, who asked if I knew anyone who might want to write a little book on tofu and thus piqued my interest; and to my indefatigable agent, Doe Coover, for once again moving an idea toward becoming a book.

This book did not appear out of nowhere, but out of the work, lives, and traditions of many people. I would especially like to acknowledge Bill Shurtleff and Aikiko Ayogi for leading the way of tofu in America with their masterful work, *The Book of Tofu*, which has long been a part of my life; to Kyung-Lim Lee for translating her Korean tofu recipes for me; to Ta Lin grocery in Albuquerque, New Mexico, for not only carrying the most delicious tofu, but for telling me how to use it; to the many Asian restaurants I've frequented in my life, starting with the Iris Cafe in Sacramento, where I first encountered tofu so many years ago as a teen foodie; and to the many cooks and authors who have inspired my own use and enjoyment of a very special food. All of you provide the shoulders on which I stand.

Contents

This anecdote appeared in the *Metropolitan Diary* in *The New York Times* while I was writing *This Can't Be Tofu!*

> *Jane Block, shopping in her local health store, placed a container of fresh tofu in her basket. A well-dressed man approached her and in a clipped British accent asked exactly what she did with the tofu. She replied that normally she put it in the refrigerator, looked at it for several weeks, and then threw it away. The man replied: "That's exactly what my wife does with it. I was hoping you had a better recipe."*

Well, for all of you whose relationship to tofu is as earnest, but as unfilled as Jane's, here are some better recipes.

I WAS EIGHT WHEN A FRIEND of my father's asked if he could use me in a film he was making about soybeans. My part was to paint a chair with a pink paint that was based on soybean oil. The film featured a lot of other friends doing things with soy-based products, but I don't recall that the soybean was ever portrayed as food, except possibly as a meat extender. In the 1950s, there wouldn't have been any mention of tofu, miso, or soy milk, for traditional soy foods were only to be found in the homes and restaurants of Japanese and Chinese Americans.

Today this is no longer the case, for we have greatly expanded our knowledge of soy foods and are now well aware of the healthful possibilities contained in the soybean, especially when made into tofu. In soy foods, especially tofu, we have a plant food that's protein dense, has no cholesterol, abounds in phytochemicals that may protect against heart disease, isoflavonoids that can help soften the effects of menopause and protect against breast cancer, and reasonable calories for those who are counting them. In short, these are the very qualities that have probably fueled your interest in soy in the first place. What I want to do is alert you to its culinary possibilities, because it's just not enough to know something's good for you, then treat it like medicine. Without tofu being understood, isn't it likely just to sit there in your refrigerator until you throw it out? There's absolutely no reason to be eating tofu with the enthusiasm usually reserved for flossing our teeth. This sad approach completely eclipses its considerable culinary possibilities, as you will discover. In addition, you'll be thrilled to discover that tofu is one of the quickest and easiest foods you can cook.

Knowing what tofu is and what its different designations mean—which type is for what and how to handle it—is important for producing good results in your kitchen. If you're unfamiliar with tofu, do spend a little time with the introductory material so that you can start off in the right direction and enjoy the results of your efforts.

IF YOU'VE NEVER ENCOUNTERED TOFU, you may feel perplexed about how to approach it. This is entirely understandable. At first glance, it's simply not like any of the other foods we eat although, with experience, you may find this isn't so. One of the best ways to become acquainted with tofu is to go to a restaurant and order a dish that has tofu, or bean curd, as it's also called. Have a plate of mapo tofu in a Chinese restaurant, or order sukiyaki in a Japanese one, where you'll also find tofu in your miso soup. In a Korean restaurant, you may have a stir-fry of beef and tofu. Many people enjoy tofu in the context of those cuisines where tofu is enough in and of itself and doesn't pretend to be something else. In fact, since working on this book, it seems that everyone I meet is eager to tell me about a wonderful little tofu dish they had in a Thai, Japanese, Korean, or Chinese restaurant.

Similarly, I've found that one of the easiest approaches to cooking tofu at home is to cook it within the traditional flavors you've already encountered in restaurants. The reason why so many of the dishes in this book use ginger, coconut, cilantro, soy sauce, and other Asian ingredients is that they go so well with the delicate, nutty flavor of tofu. It turns out that tofu is also well enhanced by curry spices and Indian cooking techniques. It rather resembles the Indian cheese called *paneer,* and, in fact, it does stand in well for paneer.

When it comes to translating tofu for a Western palate, there are two main directions you can go in. One is to be quite obvious about it. You know you're eating tofu when you bite into that Bachelor Tofu Sandwich (page 44); the surprise is that it's so good. The second is to use tofu so that it disappears. Blend it in a smoothie, whip it into mayonnaise, or add it to a cheese filling for manicotti. I've even had it in a chocolate cake. The surprise is that it's there at all; you would never know.

Another way tofu has been used, an approach that I'm not at all fond of, is when it masquerades as feta cheese in a salad, a slab of mozzarella in a lasagna, or is crumbled up to imitate hamburger. What a rude surprise when you find out that those white cubes weren't feta cheese after all! These recipes won't lead you to expect one thing, then get another. They're here simply because they taste good.

A lot of people say they don't like tofu, or don't like its texture, but my hunch is that that's a case of tofu being misunderstood. If, after trying these recipes, you find that you still don't like tofu, but want to include it in your diet, then look at the Smoothies and Shakes chapter (pages 112–118) and enjoy a lot of rich-tasting, creamy drinks.

Disappearing Tofu and Dessert

While most of the recipes in this book treat tofu as a food to be enjoyed for its own intrinsic qualities, tofu can also disappear into dishes so completely that you don't even know it's there. The success of a dessert made with tofu, a tofu mayonnaise, or tofu as feta cheese or sour cream, depends in part on where your food experiences lie. If you like the taste of traditional foods and aren't using tofu in order to avoid eggs or dairy, then including some in a standard recipe gives you the benefits of soy without giving up traditional flavors. For example, you can stir pureed silken tofu into prepared mayonnaise, or into a ricotta filling intended for manicotti, ravioli, or enchiladas, and truly not know the difference. I have a suspicious palate when it comes to substitutes, so you can trust me on this.

When it comes to desserts, you might find soy milk a bit easier to use than tofu. Soy milk can be used wherever milk is called for in a recipe, except where color is important. For example, it makes no difference in a butterscotch tapioca or chocolate pudding, but it might be off-putting in an old-fashioned vanilla custard, simply because its hue can be slightly brownish. Otherwise, soy milk can easily be used as a substitute in dishes such as in cakes and French toast.

In desserts and baked goods, use 2 ounces pureed silken tofu to replace each egg called for in pancake, muffin, quick bread, and cake recipes. Or add tofu along with the eggs, or just the egg whites, to your recipe. The tofu provides moisture and structure to baked goods, yet doesn't interfere with the flavor. It can even be included in a chocolate cake or a pumpkin pie with no one the wiser, and tofu cheesecakes have become rather popular these days. When using pureed tofu in baked goods, make sure that it's completely smooth before adding it to a batter. Any little gobbets of tofu will harden as they bake and leave their visible traces, attractive neither to the tongue nor to the eye.

Not Just for Vegetarians

Tofu is particularly beloved of vegetarians because, among its other qualities, it is an excellent protein source and it is very easy to use in vegetarian dishes. But choosing to eat more tofu doesn't mean that you have to become vegetarian. Traditionally, tofu is often combined with meat in dishes: in sukiyaki, tofu simmers with beef. Across Asia, tofu is seasoned with dried shrimp or oyster sauce, or simmered in chicken stock or *daishi no moto,* a Japanese stock made with dried bonito. If you are trying to include tofu at your table but are not a vegetarian, add it to stir-fries that you already know how to make, even if they use meat and fish. Reduce the amount of meat you use if that's what you're striving to do.

I have included some recipes that combine tofu with seafood, list both chicken and vegetable stocks as ingredients, and occasionally call for oyster sauce and fish sauce, which are excellent complementary flavorings for tofu. But for the most part, the recipes in this book are made without meat or fowl, since tofu does so well as a substitute for the protein-dense foods and is of special interest to vegetarians or those aiming to eat less meat.

Frozen Tofu

It's a common practice to freeze slabs of firm, Chinese-style tofu in order to alter its texture so that it resembles ground meat. The water in it expands as it freezes, filling the tofu with pores and pockets of air that give it a crumbly, fluffy texture when thawed. (You can quickly defrost the tofu in warm water, then squeeze out the excess moisture.) But you don't have to crumble tofu just because it's been frozen. You can defrost it and cut it into slabs, then marinate it or cook it in a saucy dish. The additional pores that it's gained in the freezer are great at pulling in a marinade or highly seasoned sauce.

As many times as I have cooked with frozen tofu, I've never found the results texturally appealing; in fact, quite the opposite. And certainly I've never been as happy with the results as when I use fresh tofu. On the whole, if you want a crumbly hamburger-like texture, you're better off starting with a fresh block of firm or extra-firm tofu packed in water, breaking it up with your hands, then drying it out in a skillet with a little oil, salt, and pepper. You'll end up with both a texture and a taste that are more appealing.

Types of Tofu

. . . .

AS IF IT'S NOT HARD ENOUGH TO REACH for your first package of tofu, which kind do you reach for? Soft or silken? Firm or extra-firm? Tofu that comes packed in water or tofu sealed in a box on a shelf far from any refrigeration? If you haven't any idea about what to choose or why, you're certainly not alone. For a lot of people this is sheer guesswork, and it needn't be.

Before reviewing the kinds of tofu, it might be helpful first to understand how tofu is made. Making tofu is not dissimilar to making simple cheeses, such as ricotta, or yogurt. The process begins with a liquid that looks just like rich whole milk, only it's made from ground soybeans. This soy milk is heated, just as cows' milk is, then it's either curdled or solidified with the addition of salts or acid.

Salts, such as nigari, magnesium chloride or calcium sulfate, work like rennet to separate the soy milk into curds and whey. The delicate curds are ladled into settling boxes that are perforated and lined with cloth. The whey drips out of the boxes, the remaining curds are pressed, and the result is tofu. The more the tofu is pressed, the firmer it becomes, and the more nutrient and calorically dense it becomes as well. The tofu is then packed in water-filled cartons. A recent addition to the market is very firm baked tofu that is packaged in oxygen-free plastic wrappers.

In a second process, thicker soy milk plus another substance, lactone, is added with the coagulant, which makes it possible for the soymilk to thicken in its container the way yogurt does. As there is no whey or any need for pressing, the resulting tofu is soft and silky, like yogurt. In fact, this type of tofu is called "silken tofu." Traditionally silken tofu can be as delicate as the most perfectly cooked custard. The Chinese shopgirl in a market where I buy an exceptionally delicate fresh silken tofu says she loves this kind best and simply eats it with a spoon. Most silken tofu, however, is sold in foil-lined aseptic cartons that keep for months unrefrigerated.

Although both the regular pressed curds and the silken tofu are labeled *soft, firm,* or *extra-firm,* silken tofu is always more delicate and smoother than tofu packed in water. Each type of tofu has its own best use. Here's what you're likely to find in your supermarket.

This tofu is made by the curds-and-whey method. It is available in individual cartons. It is packed in water, which keeps the tofu fresh. You'll find it refrigerated, either in the produce section of your market near the Asian vegetables or in the dairy case. Some brands are Nasoya, Azumaya, Quong Hop, if you live in the San Francisco Bay Area, White Wave, and others. While there are some national brands, every part of the country has a few small local factories that produce tofu. My preference is for the Japanese brands; I find their textures and flavors superior. I find some of the newer non-Asian brands tend to be a little grainier, but like everything, it's a matter of personal taste and how you plan to use the tofu.

Usually this type of tofu comes in one block, but sometimes it comes in four smaller blocks, each weighing about 5 ounces. This is most likely to be true when you buy Chinese brands in an Asian market. In general, the cartons weigh between 14 and 20 ounces. Usually, one carton is enough for two to four servings—two, if you really like tofu.

Firm or Regular: Referred to by either name, I think of this as my all-purpose tofu. It's strong enough to withstand frying, sautéing, and grilling, but tender enough to take the place of soft tofu. Even when fried until crisp on the outside, it will be creamy on the inside. It's not quite as smooth as the soft tofu, nor is it as grainy as the extra-firm. It is the tofu I've used most often in this book. If you're going to buy tofu but don't know how you're going to use it, you'll be safest buying regular or firm tofu.

Soft: Use this kind of tofu when you want to serve very simple tofu dishes that have nothing more than a little sauce or garnish, tofu that's to appear in salads, or tofu that you intend to scramble like eggs or *with* eggs. Soft tofu is also good in a smoothie, added to baked goods, or used in place of mayonnaise and other creamy-textured sauces and dips. Soft tofu has the most delicate taste and custardlike texture. As you would expect, it requires more careful handling, unless it's to be pureed.

Extra-firm: This tofu has been pressed longer than soft or firm tofu. This is the tofu you can marinate forever, throw on a grill without fear of it's breaking apart, or use where you want the crumbly texture of ground pork or hamburger, although the firm tofu will work, too. In short, you can handle it roughly. When people say they don't like the texture of tofu, I am fairly sure that extra-firm is the kind they're referring to, because it's a little coarse and lacks the delicacy of softer tofu. However, it's ideal when you need tofu that won't fall apart or when you're planning to break it into crumbles, as in the Green "Chorizo" on page 105.

Silken Tofu

Made like yogurt, this tofu sets into a single smooth unit; there is no whey. Most often, silken tofu comes aseptically packed in a 10-ounce box that needs no refrigeration. While many stores feature silken tofu in the produce section, it can also be found on the aisle where curry pastes, noodles, and soy sauce are sold. It is not surrounded with water, though once opened, if you haven't managed to use it all at once, you can keep it by covering it with cold water. It will keep this way for 2 to 3 days.

Although silken tofu comes labeled *soft, firm,* and *extra-firm,* even the extra-firm is fairly soft and tender. However, it can successfully be fried and will fall apart only marginally in a stir-fry. Soft silken tofu tastes good and looks beautiful when floating in a miso soup, and firm and extra-firm both work well mingling among salad leaves with their pungent dressings. When adding silken tofu to salads, I often simmer it first in salted water for 2 minutes, which improves the flavor and firms the texture.

The soft silken tofu is ideal for pureeing and using in dishes where you plan to have it disappear, as in salad dressings, mayonnaise, or smoothies, or if you wish to scramble it with eggs or treat it like the Indian cheese, paneer. However you can use firm and extra-firm silken tofus as well.

Draining: Draining simply means pouring off the water that the tofu is packaged in. Pressing refers to wrapping it in cloth or paper towels or letting it sit on toweling to force out the excess water within. The reasons for pressing the water out of tofu are:

1. To make room for other liquids and seasonings to be absorbed, such as marinades and spice rubs
2. To prevent excess spattering when deep-frying tofu
3. To prevent diluting sauces and dressings

However, you don't have to fret about this, nor do you have to do it every time. Generally, I find that tofu can simply sit on some toweling while I'm assembling other ingredients, and that's plenty of time to remove excess water. For tofu that's to be deep-fried, you have to do a serious pressing or the water will spurt dangerously in the oil. If you're not deep-frying tofu, look to the simpler methods that follow.

Serious Pressing: Wrap an entire piece of drained tofu in an absorbent dish towel. Set the tofu on a cutting board and weight it down with something heavy, like a large can of tomatoes. Rest one end of the board on a plate or something else so that the board with the weighted tofu is tilted toward the sink. The excess water will drain off and flow into the sink. Leave for 20 to 30 minutes.

Towel Drying: This method is especially good for sliced tofu that's going to be shallow-fried. Use a cloth dish towel or several layers of paper towels. Lay the sliced tofu on the toweling, cover it with a second layer, and press gently to wick off the excess moisture. Leave it like this while you prepare the rest of your ingredients.

Pan Drying: This process both dries and firms the tofu so that it won't fall apart in a stir-fry. Slice or cube the tofu without pressing or towel drying first, then put it in a nonstick skillet over medium-high heat, adding a little oil if you wish. The water in the tofu will evaporate and eventually the tofu will brown slightly, even if you haven't added any oil to the pan. This will both dry and firm the tofu.

Oven Drying: Place sliced or cubed tofu in a very lightly oiled pie plate and cook at 375°F until all the water has evaporated and the tofu has a nice, slightly firm feel to it when pressed with your finger. This will take 20 to 25 minutes at 375°. After 10 to 12 minutes, the tofu will have released a lot of water. Carefully pour it off, then return the tofu to the oven to finish drying.

The Myth of Marinating

Along with the notion that tofu will become whatever you wish by virtue of its seasonings comes the idea of the marinade, the liquid means of transformation. I have always felt that marinades are terribly overrated, and that they don't really accomplish much except to flavor the very outside of the tofu itself. When I was the chef at Greens restaurant, we used to keep blocks of firm Chinese tofu submerged for days in an extremely strong marinade of red wine, mustard, dried mushrooms, soy sauce, and other ingredients, but it never did much more than affect the appearance and taste of the tofu's outermost surfaces. When we cut into it, it was pure white, the marinade clearly never having penetrated the tofu.

A more effective use for a marinade is as a cooking liquid. Pour it over the tofu as it cooks and the marinade will reduce and leave a lustrous, flavorful sheen. I think you'll be very happy with the results. Here's the basic method:

1. Drain, then slice or cube the tofu. No need to use the serious pressing method, just blot dry the tofu to remove some of the water. Assemble your marinade ingredients. Many marinade recipes are similar to each other, consisting of garlic, ginger, scallions, soy sauce, sugar, and maybe some molasses or dark vinegar. The sugar or molasses give the tofu its glossy sheen.

2. Heat a large nonstick or cast-iron skillet. Spray the skillet with peanut oil from your own mister, or a spray such as Oriental Mist, add the tofu and sear until golden on both sides. Even if you don't use any oil, the tofu will color, but it's best if it colors a lot and for that you need some oil. If you use enough oil to shallow-fry, the tofu will also get a crisp, golden crust.

3. When the tofu is nicely colored, pour the marinade over the tofu and continue cooking until it has reduced to a glaze. As the marinade cooks down, the sugars caramelize, leaving behind some very delectable tofu. You can simply serve the tofu as is, or garnish it with toasted sesame seeds and slivered scallions. You can also slice the tofu and add it to a noodle or rice salad or a stir-fry.

Silken and Soft Regular Tofu

These techniques, which can be used with all grades of silken tofu as well as soft regular tofu, firm the texture, which keeps it from falling apart when cooked. The cooking and the salt also round out the flavor. I routinely use this technique with silken tofu that I'm going to cook further, and when I use tofu in salads.

Simmering: Bring 6 cups water in a wide skillet to the boil. Add 1 teaspoon sea salt, then lower the heat so that the water is barely simmering. Add the tofu. Simmer small cubes for 1 to 2 minutes; larger cubes for 4 to 5 minutes. Gently remove the tofu with a strainer and set it on a towel to drain for several minutes. Once dried, this tofu will be fine for gentle frying.

Steeping: Bring 6 cups water in a wide skillet to a boil. Add 1 teaspoon salt, then turn off the heat. Add the tofu and let it steep for 3 to 5 minutes. Remove with a flat strainer. If you wish to cool the tofu, lower the strainer into a bowl of cold water, then turn the tofu onto a towel until needed.

I have strived to make this book an easy one to use, one that doesn't rely on exotic ingredients or techniques. While I enjoy tofu in the context of traditional Asian cuisines, I'm not an expert in these cuisines and don't mean to send you scurrying for the esoteric ingredients that give them their true characters. If you wish to learn about a cuisine in more depth, I know that you'll turn, as will I, to the real experts. For this book, most of the Asian ingredients called for are available in your supermarket. Yet there is much more to discover if you set about exploring Asian grocery stores. (I say Asian because often a single market caters to the entire pan-Asian community by selling foods from Japan, China, Vietnam, Thailand, India, Korea.) While row after row of unfamiliar foods with unrecognizable labels can be daunting, there are many useful ingredients to be ferreted out that go especially well with tofu, starting with the tofu itself.

I find the most delicious tofu in Asian markets, where it tends to be extremely fresh. I am always happy when I find extra-firm Chinese tofu floating in large buckets of water, the tofu white, the water clear and clean smelling. This is tofu that's made, sold, and probably eaten the same day, and the difference in flavor between this and packaged tofu is significant. Those who eat tofu regularly value the high quality of fresh tofu and usually shop in markets where the turnover supports its daily fabrication. If you're not well acquainted with the store where you see such tofu, ask when and where it was made. Don't forget to use your nose: fresh tofu should never smell sour. It should be sweet and slightly nutty.

My Asian market also carries a variety of regional brands that are not available in most supermarkets. This tofu, which often comes in large weights of about 20 ounces each, is a more practical size for four servings. I've also found a very delicate tofu that can be eaten like custard or blended into smoothies or whatever else you wish. You can also buy little kits that allow you to make your own tofu quite easily, if you're ever curious to give it a try.

Because tofu is so good with Asian seasonings, these markets are good places to pick up basics such as rice wine and rice wine vinegar, thin soy sauce, mushroom soy sauce, coconut milk, roasted sesame and peanut oils, fish sauce, oyster sauce, black and white sesame seeds, and other frequently used ingredients. Sambal oelek, a red chili paste, provides an interesting hot accent to dishes. You can also find all kinds of noodles, from rice sticks and mung bean threads to Chinese egg noodles and Vietnamese rice paper pancakes. Search out items such as Korean barbecue sauce, black bean sauce, chili paste with soybeans, dried mushrooms, hoisin sauce, plum sauce, and other delicious condiments. Prepared sauces, for mapo tofu or Szechuan spicy noodles, allow you to make a meal in moments. In the Indian aisle of the market, or in an Indian grocery, if your area has one, there are spices for making curry mixtures and masalas, plus chutneys and tamarind paste. Japanese markets offer delicate somen, udon, and earthy-tasting soba, or buckwheat, noodles along with delicious, dark Kadoya sesame oil and *kombu* and other sea greens. While I've never tried them, there are seemingly endless displays of packaged sauces that look enticing, to which you add water. They may be delicious with tofu.

Many books have been written on all branches of Asian cooking to help you make sense of what these exotic markets offer. Use these guides, and you'll significantly widen your cooking vocabulary, especially for tofu.

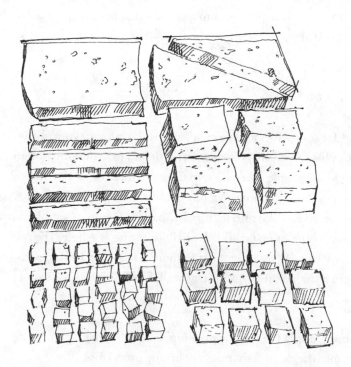

Simple, Basic Tofu

THE FOLLOWING SEVEN RECIPES ARE SIMPLE, basic approaches that will allow you to cook tofu with particular ease and speed. The results can be enjoyed immediately (try Fried Tofu, below, with a peanut sauce or sprinkled with salt), incorporated into other dishes (see Tofu and Mushrooms Braised in a Sweet-and-Sour Sauce, on page 90), or just used as techniques in other recipes.

While the smoking technique is not quite as speedy as searing and glazing, it does provide you with barbecued tofu that can go right into a sandwich or become part of another dish where smoky flavor and meaty texture are desired.

About Frying Tofu

Many people prefer tofu when it has a crisp, golden exterior. Frying always makes everything taste better, of course, plus the pretty golden exterior makes tofu that much more attractive as an ingredient. Because a lot of people don't want to deep-fry these days, I've not called for this method except in a few recipes. You can, however, buy chunks of deep-fried tofu in Asian markets.

Tofu can also be given color and texture by shallow-frying or simply browning in a nonstick or castiron skillet with little or no fat added. Shallow-frying also helps the spice coatings used in some dishes to do their work of flavoring the tofu more effectively. Frying not only gives tofu an attractive color and crisp surface, it firms it up as well. Don't hesitate to season the tofu with a little salt and pepper.

Deep-Frying: First, apply the serious pressing technique (page 7) to a block of firm or extra-firm tofu, then cut it into the desired shapes. Blot up any excess moisture with paper towels. Heat two to three cups of peanut or vegetable oil in a deep-sided pot or skillet. When the oil is hot enough to quickly sizzle a piece of tofu, add several pieces of tofu to the pot. They will cluster together and tend to fuse in the oil, so use tongs or chopsticks to separate them as they cook. Fry until golden, but don't let them get brown or the tofu will be too hard. Remove the tofu and drain it on paper toweling. Use these tofu pieces in other dishes, or salt them and serve with a peanut sauce or other dipping sauce as an appetizer.

Shallow-Frying: Dry the tofu thoroughly, but not fanatically. Heat enough oil to cover the bottom of a skillet by about ¼ inch or slightly less. When hot, add the tofu in a single layer and cook over medium-high heat, turning occasionally, until golden, about 5 minutes on each side. Drain on paper towels if desired. You can use the tofu in stir-fries or other dishes, or return it all to the pan and add whatever sauce or flavoring you desire.

Pan-Browning: Because tofu already has a fair amount of fat in it, if you add sliced or cubed tofu to a dry non-stick skillet as described on page 8, it will eventually color a bit, turning pale gold. If you don't mind a little fat, misting the pan lightly with peanut oil will bring out more color. Add a pinch or two of sea salt and some pepper when you're done. As with any other foods, salt and pepper make tofu taste better.

Commercially Prepared Deep-Fried Tofu

Sometimes called *age,* these pieces of deep-fried tofu can be found packaged a dozen or so to a pack in Chinese and Japanese grocery stores. (Look for it in the refrigerated cases or freezer.) I often include one or two of these pieces, slivered or diced, along with my regular tofu, as a flavor accent. They have a great chewy texture and an attractive golden surface.

Before using deep-fried tofu, dip it in a pan of boiling water for several seconds, or pour the water over it to remove some of the frying oil. Thinly slice the tofu and add the pieces to stir fries or fried rice, or cut into larger pieces and simmer in a stew along with fresh tofu.

1 carton firm tofu, drained

2 tablespoons olive or vegetable oil

3 tablespoons Worcestershire sauce, steak sauce, or tamari

Salt and freshly ground black pepper

SERVES 3 TO 4

1.   Slice the tofu crosswise into 6 or 8 pieces, $\frac{1}{2}$-inch thick or slightly less. Blot with paper towels.

2.   Heat the oil in a cast-iron skillet. When hot, add the tofu and fry over medium-high heat until golden. Turn and cook the second side, about 10 minutes in all. Pour over the Worcestershire sauce and continue cooking until it evaporates, leaving the tofu nicely glazed and seasoned. Salt lightly and season with plenty of pepper. ●

This is fast and easy. Eat it as is or add any condiments of the mustard-mayo-horseradish variety.

Seared Tofu with Chives and Pepper

MAKES 6 TO 8 PIECES

Utterly straightforward, fast, and good, you can vary it by using olive oil and, another herb, such as tarragon or oregano, in place of the cilantro. With the soy and sesame, it becomes something of an East-West combination, but one that works.

1 carton firm tofu, drained

1 tablespoon peanut or vegetable oil

3 tablespoons soy sauce

1 scallion, thinly sliced on the diagonal

1 tablespoon finely minced chives

Pinch red pepper flakes

4 teaspoons chopped cilantro

1 tablespoon toasted sesame seeds

Sea salt and freshly ground black pepper

1. Cut the tofu into slabs about ½ inch thick or a little less and set on paper toweling while you assemble the rest of the ingredients. Blot the tops as well.

2. Heat a nonstick skillet, then lightly coat it with the oil. When hot, add the tofu and cook over medium-high heat until golden but still tender, 4 to 5 minutes. Turn and cook the second side. Sprinkle the soy sauce over the tofu and turn off the heat. It will quickly evaporate.

3. Scatter the scallion, chives, pepper flakes, cilantro, and sesame seeds over the top, then season with salt and pepper. Serve immediately.

1 carton firm or extra-firm tofu

2 large garlic cloves, coarsely chopped

2 tablespoons fresh lime or lemon juice

1/2 cup soy sauce

1 tablespoon molasses

2 teaspoons roasted peanut or dark sesame oil

2 tablespoons chopped cilantro

Salt and freshly ground black pepper

1 to 2 tablespoons vegetable oil

1. Drain the tofu, cut it into the shapes and sizes you desire, and set on paper toweling to drain. Blot well.

2. While the tofu is draining, combine the next 6 ingredients in a small bowl. Season with a few pinches of salt and plenty of pepper.

3. Heat a large cast-iron skillet or nonstick pan and film with a tablespoon of oil. When hot, add the tofu and cook over medium-high heat, without disturbing, until crisp and golden, about 7 minutes. Turn and cook on the other side, adding more oil if necessary.

4. Pour in the marinade and shuffle the pan back and forth to coat the tofu. Reduce the heat to medium and cook until the sauce is syrupy and the tofu is glazed. Don't let it cook so long that it gets sticky.

Glazed Tofu

SERVES 3 TO 4

This is a basic technique you can use with any marinade. Glazing is much more effective than marinating; it couldn't be easier, plus there's a lot you can do with this recipe. You can cut the tofu into strips or small cubes, then toss them into hot or cold Chinese noodles. Cut the tofu into 1 inch cubes, skewer them and serve as an appetizer with the Peanut Sauce on page 32. You can also cut the tofu into larger triangles and serve them as a main course, again with peanut sauce, a scattering of lemon thyme leaves or slivered scallions.

Grilled Tofu

After much experience I'm convinced that all the marinating in the world doesn't do as much for tofu as we'd like it to. The marinade doesn't really penetrate or transform the tofu. What you might do, however, to give the tofu some luster and a bit of flavor on the surface, is simply to brush it with any of the sauces mentioned above or some similar sauce. While you're at it, grill some onion rings as well. Regardless of the sauce you use, they'll be great on top or alongside (see Note).

1 carton extra-firm or firm tofu, drained

3/4 cup of any of the following: soy sauce or tamari, teriyaki sauce, steak sauce, Worcestershire sauce, commercial barbecue sauce, or Korean barbecue sauce

Salt and freshly ground black pepper

1. Slice the tofu into ½ inch slabs. Brush it with any of the sauces and season with salt and pepper.

2. Preheat the grill. Make sure the grill rack is clean and oiled. You can add wood chips or rosemary twigs to the flames for their fragrant smoke.

3. Cook the tofu until lightly browned, 5 to 7 minutes. Turn 45 degrees for cross-hatched lines, if desired, then turn and cook on the second side as well. Brush with additional sauce as it cooks. Just take care not to overcook it; tofu can dry out. Serve with accompaniments such as sambals, chutneys, or salsas.

Note: For onion rings, slice a large, peeled red or yellow onion into ½ inch rounds. Brush with olive oil and season with salt and pepper. Secure the rings with a couple of toothpicks so they won't fall apart. Grill on both sides until lightly marked and slightly softened.

1 carton firm or extra-firm tofu, drained
   and sliced into 6 slabs
3 tablespoons butter or oil
5 teaspoons Worcestershire sauce

   •

Spice Rub
3 tablespoons paprika
1 tablespoon freshly ground black
   pepper

1 tablespoon sugar
2 teaspoons dry mustard
1/2 teaspoon cayenne pepper or ground
   chipotle chile

   •

Approximately 1/2 cup barbecue sauce

Smoked Tofu with Barbecue Sauce

MAKES 6 PIECES

1. Press the tofu so that the slices are quite dry.

2. Melt the butter and stir in the Worcestershire sauce. Give it a stir, then brush it over the tofu, covering both sides.

3. Combine the ingredients for the rub and sprinkle them over the sauced tofu. Don't be tempted to make this too thick or it won't taste good in the end.

4. Scatter 2 tablespoons wood chips in the bottom of a stovetop smoker. Lightly oil the rack and place the tofu on it. Close the top and cook over low heat for 15 minutes. Open, brush tops of the tofu generously with barbecue sauce, and cook 15 minutes more. When done the tofu should be firm but offer a little resistance when pressed. Don't let it get hard, but if it still feels just a little too soft, brush it once more with barbecue sauce and cook 10 to 15 minutes longer, or until done.

The first time I put tofu in a smoker, not much happened. As with a marinade, the smoky flavor stayed mainly on the surface. But then I tried using some ideas from Smoke and Spice, *the smoker's bible, by Bill and Cheryl Jamison, and got some very different results. With a Cameron stovetop smoker this couldn't be easier—or more effective. Keep in mind that the tofu just isn't going to be wet and juicy like a barbecued brisket, even if the flavor is good. So what to do with it? I put it in a white roll with extra sauce and some sliced onions (you could smoke those, too, while you're at it). Coleslaw on the side, of course. Chunk up any leftovers and add them to a pot of chili.*

There's enough spice rub here for two cartons of tofu, but you'll need to double the amount of butter and Worcestershire sauce.

Grilled, Braised, or Broiled Tofu with Tamarind Barbecue Sauce

SERVES 3 TO 4

Regardless of which cooking method you choose, you'll have the best results if you fry the tofu first—it will have a better texture, appearance, and flavor. Extra-firm tofu can withstand the slightly rougher handling on the grill, but the firm tofu will work, too. Since there's likely to be extra sauce, you can double the amount of tofu.

1 or 2 cartons firm or extra-firm tofu, drained

1 to 2 tablespoons peanut or vegetable oil

•

Tamarind Barbecue Sauce

¹/₃ cup brown sugar

¹/₄ cup balsamic vinegar

1 tablespoon strong red wine vinegar

¹/₂ cup water or chicken stock

¹/₂ cup diced fresh tomatoes or canned diced tomatoes in puree

1 teaspoon hot mustard

1 tablespoon tamarind paste

1 tablespoon roasted peanut oil

Freshly ground black pepper

1. Cut the tofu crosswise or lengthwise into slabs about ½ inch thick or a bit less. Set on paper toweling while you mix together the ingredients for the sauce.

2. Heat a nonstick or cast-iron skillet and add 1 tablespoon vegetable oil. When hot, add the tofu and fry until golden. Turn, adding more oil to the pan if needed, and fry on the second side. Turn off the heat.

3. Combine the sauce ingredients in a medium saucepan. Bring to a boil and stir to dissolve the tamarind paste. Boil until thickened and the surface is covered with bubbles, 4 to 5 minutes.

To Grill: Brush the tofu with the marinade. Make a fire or preheat the grill, making sure that the grill rack is very clean. Brush or spray it with oil. Place the tofu on the grill and cook without turning until browned, about 5 minutes, depending on the heat of the fire (you may have to pick up a corner and check). Turn the tofu 45 degrees and cook a few minutes more to get a nice set of grill marks. As the tofu cooks, continue to brush the sauce over it to keep it moist. Heat any extra marinade and serve it on the side.

To Broil: Preheat the broiler and brush the fried tofu very generously with the sauce. You won't need to use it all. Broil about 5 inches from the heat. When bubbly and reduced, turn the tofu, brush it again with sauce, and broil the second side. Heat the extra sauce and serve it with the tofu and/or an accompaniment.

To Braise: Once the tofu is golden, add half the marinade and let it cook over medium-high heat, sloshing it over the tofu, until well reduced and the tofu is burnished but not dry, about 4 to 5 minutes.

THE SECRET FOR MAKING TOFU WORK as an appetizer is to make dishes with intense flavors and interesting textures. Using dipping sauces, deep frying, having crunchy coatings of sesame seeds or pepper, and allying tofu with lively ingredients, such as ginger, all contribute to making successful appetizers that can be eaten with the fingers or from a toothpick.

Frying isn't always a must, however. If you enjoy the delicate flavor of fresh, soft tofu, there are some other options, such as serving it chilled with little bowls of scallions, soy sauce, and grated ginger, a remarkably simple dish and one that's more typically Japanese. One appetizer I thoroughly enjoy is *hiya-yakko*—cubes of impeccably fresh tofu served in a bowl of water and ice and accompanied by a very lively dipping sauce. This is utterly cool and soothing on a hot August evening.

Spring Rolls with Shredded Cabbage, Mushrooms, and Tofu

MAKES 12 TO 15 PLUMP ROLLS

Who doesn't like crisp spring rolls? Serve these with little bowls of hot mustard for dipping.

1 small napa cabbage

Salt and freshly ground black pepper

5 dried shiitake mushrooms

2 pieces commercial deep-fried tofu (optional)

1 box extra-firm silken tofu or 1/2 carton soft tofu

2 teaspoons roasted peanut oil

1/4 cup chopped scallions, including half of the greens

1/2 pound fresh mushrooms, brown, white, or shiitake, chopped

1 tablespoon minced garlic

2 heaping tablespoons minced ginger

2 teaspoons rice wine vinegar

1/2 teaspoon ground Szechuan peppercorns

1 tablespoon soy sauce

1/4 cup chopped cilantro, plus cilantro sprigs for garnish

15 egg roll wrappers

2 cups peanut oil, for frying

1. Quarter the cabbage lengthwise, then slice it crosswise into thin strips. Measure 5 cups, place in a colander, and sprinkle lightly with salt. Toss and set aside.

2. Boil several cups of water. Pour half over the deep-fried tofu, if using, to rid it of the extra oil. Pour just enough to cover the dried mushrooms and let steep for 15 minutes. Squeeze them dry, remove and discard the stems, and thinly slice the caps.

3. Cut the fried tofu into slivers and the fresh tofu into tiny cubes. Bring 1 quart water to a boil in a 10 to 12 inch skillet, add 1 teaspoon salt, then lower the heat to a simmer. Carefully add the fresh tofu and cook for 2 minutes. Remove and set on a cloth towel to drain.

4. Heat the oil in a wok or nonstick skillet. When hot, add the scallions and fresh and dried mushrooms. Sauté quickly over brisk heat for 1 minute, then scrape the mixture into a bowl. Squeeze the moisture out of the cabbage and add it to the scallion mixture along with the remaining ingredients. Taste, adjust salt, add pepper, and make sure the seasonings are bright and lively.

5. Lay an egg roll wrapper on the counter facing you on the diagonal. Place about 3 tablespoons filling in the center. Brush a strip of water around the edges, then fold the bottom up, the sides over, and roll. Repeat until all the filling is used.

6. Heat 2 cups peanut oil in a wok or skillet. When hot enough to sizzle a corner of a wrapper, add a roll and fry, turning once, until golden and crisp. Remove to drain on a paper towel and repeat until all are done. Cut them in half on the diagonal, arrange on a platter, and garnish with long sprigs of cilantro. Serve with hot mustard for dipping.

Napa Cabbage Rolls with Gingered Tofu and Peanut Mince

MAKES ABOUT 25 PACKETS

Pale and pretty napa cabbage leaves are rolled around peanut-studded, gingered tofu and served as appetizers. Vietnamese rice papers could also be used as wrappers. Serve with a peanut sauce, either a commercial sauce or the recipe on page 32, diluted with a little water to dipping consistency.

Gingered Tofu and Peanut Mince (page 27)

25 napa cabbage leaves, at least 6 inches long

Peanut Sauce (page 32)

1. Prepare the gingered tofu and peanut mince and let it cool.

2. Remove the tough stem ends from the napa cabbage by cutting out a "V" shape. Dip the leaves, a few at a time, into boiling water for 30 seconds, then spread them on a clean kitchen towel to dry.

3. Mound 1 tablespoon of the filling at the broadest part of each leaf, then fold over the sides and roll, tucking in the sides as you go. Arrange on a serving plate, seam side down, with bowls of peanut sauce for dipping.

1 teaspoon tamarind paste

2 1/2 tablespoons barley malt syrup or light brown sugar

1 carton firm or extra-firm tofu, drained, wrapped in a towel, and pressed (page 7)

1/2 cup finely sliced deep-fried tofu (optional)

2 tablespoons roasted peanut oil

1 heaping tablespoon minced garlic

4 large shallots, thinly sliced

1/4 cup finely minced ginger

Salt and freshly ground black pepper

1/2 cup roasted, unsalted peanuts, coarsely chopped

1/2 cup chopped cilantro, plus cilantro leaves for garnish

1 bunch spinach, leaves only, chopped into large pieces

4 scallions, including a few inches of the greens, thinly sliced

Gingered Tofu and Peanut Mince

MAKES ABOUT 3 1/2 CUPS

This crunchy dish looks like ground pork laced with dark green spinach leaves. In fact, you could mix some pork with the tofu, but it's quite good just as it is. Amazingly, the large amount of ginger doesn't overwhelm, and leftovers keep for days. Nothing if not versatile, gingered tofu can be spooned over rice, tossed with Chinese egg noodles, scattered over a noodle cake, and used as a filling for spring rolls, wontons, or lettuce or cabbage leaves.

1. Mash and dissolve the tamarind paste into 1/2 cup boiling water. If it doesn't dissolve evenly, use a rubber scraper to force it through a strainer. Stir in the barley malt syrup. Crumble the tofu with your hands. It should resemble ground meat, but don't worry about making the pieces even in size.

2. Heat a skillet or wok, then add 1 tablespoon oil. When hot and fragrant, add the garlic and shallots and stir-fry for about 1 minute. Remove to a bowl.

3. Return the pan to the heat, add the remaining oil and when hot, add the tofu. Stir-fry, breaking up any larger chunks, until it's firm and dry. Add the diluted tamarind, cooked garlic and shallots, and ginger. Season with 1 teaspoon salt and cook for about 3 minutes. Add the peanuts and cilantro, and season well with pepper. Remove to a bowl.

4. Add the spinach to the pan with a pinch of salt, and stir-fry until wilted. Pour off any juices, then return the tofu mixture to the pan, add the scallions, and toss well. Taste for salt and season with more pepper, if desired. Mound in a bowl or on a platter and garnish with cilantro sprigs.

Fried Tofu Skewers with Sweet-and-Spicy Dipping Sauce

1 carton firm tofu, drained
Vegetable oil, for frying
1/3 cup rice wine vinegar
1/4 cup sugar
1/2 teaspoon salt
1 teaspoon red pepper flakes

3 tablespoons roasted cashews or peanuts, finely chopped
2 scallions, including an inch or so of the greens, thinly sliced
1 tablespoon minced cilantro leaves, plus cilantro sprigs for garnish

SERVES 4 TO 6

Deep-frying the tofu will give it the chewiest texture, but you can also shallow-fry it in a few tablespoons of oil until golden and crisp, or fry it in a dry non-stick skillet until firm, although this won't yield the crispness that makes the dish so nice. Just remember that if you plan to deep-fry, press out as much water as possible beforehand so that the tofu doesn't splatter.

Serve the golden tofu mounded on a plate with tooth-picks on the side and a bowl of the cashew-laden dipping sauce. Or skewer a few pieces on small bamboo sticks, stack them log cabin–style on the plate, and pour the sauce over them.

1. Press the tofu for at least 15 minutes, according to the instructions on page 7, if you're deep-frying. Cut the tofu so that you end up with about sixteen 1-inch cubes or triangles. Tofu comes in different shapes and sizes, and exact measurements aren't always easy to determine, but aim for generous, bite-sized pieces. Blot again with paper towels, once it's cut, to wick up any excess moisture.

2. Meanwhile, combine the vinegar, sugar, and salt in a sauce pan and simmer until bubbles appear all over the surface and the mixture looks slightly syrupy. Remove from the heat and add the remaining ingredients. Place in a serving bowl.

3. Fry the tofu according to the method you wish to use, then set briefly on toweling to drain. Heap the tofu on a plate or skewer it, garnish with pretty sprigs of cilantro, and serve with the sweet-and-spicy sauce.

1 carton firm tofu

¼ cup dark sesame oil

2 tablespoons soy sauce

Juice of 1 lime

1½ teaspoons cornstarch

½ cup light peanut oil, for frying

½ cup or more black or white
   sesame seeds

Sea salt

Freshly ground black pepper

Crunchy Sesame Tofu

SERVES 6

1. Press the bulk of the water out of the tofu by wrapping it in cloth or paper toweling and setting a heavy object on top for 10 minutes or so. Then, slice it lengthwise into narrow slabs about ⅜ inch thick, and cut each slab into strips, about ⅜ inch wide. Lift them with a spatula onto fresh paper towels and cover with a second layer of towels to wick away any excess moisture.

2. Mix the sesame oil, soy sauce, lime juice, and cornstarch together in a glass pie plate. Gently add the tofu pieces, using a rubber scraper to turn them once so that they're coated with the marinade. Set aside for 30 minutes to several hours.

3. Place a cast-iron skillet on the stove over medium heat for 3 to 4 minutes. While it's heating, sprinkle half the sesame seeds over a large plate. Lift the tofu out of its marinade, letting any oil remain in the pan, and set it on the sesame seeds. Sprinkle the remaining seeds over the top.

4. Add the peanut oil to the heated skillet. As soon as it's hot enough to sizzle a piece of tofu, add 6 or 7 pieces and fry until dark gold and firm, 2 to 3 minutes, turning them as they cook so that they brown on all sides. Remove the finished pieces to paper toweling to drain and continue frying.

5. When all the pieces are fried, mound them on a pretty plate and season with sea salt and freshly ground pepper. Serve right away.

Nibble on these hot crunchy pieces before a meal, or toss them while hot into a spinach or watercress salad. There is a bit of oil in this recipe—the dark flavorful sesame oil in the marinade, and the peanut oil for frying—which is why I suggest them as an appetizer rather than as a main course. However, by the time you've finished, you'll be convinced that a good part of the oil has stayed behind—in the marinating dish, in the frying pan, but mostly over your stove. It does splatter, so don't wear your good clothes while frying.

Peppered Tofu Crisps

SERVES 6 TO 8

These dark, crispy, piquant bites can be served alone or dipped into virtually any sauce from soy sauce to balsamic vinegar to mayonnaise. They're also a very good addition to the Warm Red Cabbage Salad on page 39. If you don't want to fry all the tofu at once, it will keep, refrigerated, in its marinade for several days.

1 carton firm or extra-firm tofu

2 tablespoons soy sauce

1 teaspoon freshly ground black pepper

1/2 teaspoon red pepper flakes or ground red chile

1 teaspoon sea salt

2 tablespoons rice wine or sherry

1 tablespoon cornstarch

1 tablespoon flour

1/2 cup chopped cilantro or parsley

2 cups peanut oil, for frying

1. Cut the tofu crosswise into slabs 3/4 to 1 inch thick, then lay them on several thicknesses of paper towels. Cover with additional towels and press firmly to absorb the water. Cut it into cubes and put them in a bowl. Toss with the soy sauce, black pepper, red pepper flakes, and salt.

2. Mix the rice wine with the cornstarch and flour. Pour it over the seasoned tofu and toss well. Add the cilantro and toss once more.

3. Heat the oil in a heavy 8-inch skillet until it sizzles when a piece of tofu is added. Fry about 8 pieces at a time until golden, then scoop them out and drain on paper toweling. Fry as many pieces as you wish to serve, set them on a plate or in a napkin-lined basket, and serve right away.

1 carton firm tofu
Peanut Sauce (page 32)
1 cup peanut oil, for frying
Salt

1.   Drain, then wrap the tofu and press it well. It should be quite dry since you'll be deep-frying it. (In the meantime, make the peanut sauce.) Cut the tofu into cubes about 3/4 inch across.

2.   Heat the oil in a cast-iron skillet until hot enough to sizzle a piece of tofu. Add the tofu, 6 or 7 pieces at a time, and fry until golden but not brown. Turn them so that they color on all sides, then remove to paper toweling to drain. Sprinkle with salt and remove them to a serving dish.

3.   Serve with the peanut sauce in a communal bowl or individual bowls and provide toothpicks for skewering and dipping.

Deep-frying gives the tofu a golden crust and a soft interior, which is especially appealing when the tofu is skewered and dipped in a pungent peanut sauce. If deep-frying isn't something you want to do, you can shallow-fry the tofu or simply brown it in a dry, or lightly oiled, skillet. The textural contrast won't be as evident, but with the peanut sauce on board, it will still be very good.

Peanut Sauce

MAKES ABOUT 1 CUP

This smooth, peanuty sauce can be used as a dip for deep-fried tofu, or as a dressing for noodles, served hot or cold. It keeps for weeks in the refrigerator, and will thicken over time. Thin it with some of the noodle cooking water, stock, or even coconut milk, which will give a noticeable change in flavor, of course.

1/2 cup peanut butter, chunky or smooth, preferably unsweetened

1 large garlic clove, coarsely chopped

3 tablespoons regular or thin soy sauce

2 tablespoons balsamic or Chinese black vinegar

1 tablespoon brown sugar

1/8 teaspoon cayenne pepper or more, to taste

1/4 teaspoon salt

1/2 cup hot water

1. Combine all the ingredients in a food processor, except the water, and puree until smooth. Gradually pour in the water. Taste for salt and cayenne, adding more if necessary. ●

BECAUSE TOFU IS SUCH A VERSATILE INGREDIENT, it isn't limited to any single preparation. In salads and sandwiches, for example, tofu often appears as the main ingredient and is usually identifiable as such, but not always. Sauces, on the other hand, tend to use tofu in a more discreet manner, concealing its identity by mingling it with herbs, garlic, mayonnaise and such.

While tofu might appear as mock chicken, you can also reverse the order, using tofu in a dressing to spoon over poached chicken or fish. Other simple preparations feature tofu in a salad with chilled buckwheat noodles or finely shredded napa cabbage in its purest form: uncooked and seasoned with the simplest of sauces. On the other hand, little cubes of glazed, peppered tofu show up in a warm cabbage salad.

Tofu's guises are many. Whether simply browned in a skillet with a dash of Worcestershire sauce or more elaborately seasoned with an oregano-pesto coating, tofu makes a robust sandwich filling that goes great with mayonnaise, mustard, tomatoes, or sautéed onions. It can also disappear into such familiar sandwich fillings for falafel or croquettes, while a curried crumbled tofu dish makes a new and unexpected filling for pita bread.

As for sauces, I find that tofu (preferably silken) works best in mayonnaise-type sauces that are white and creamy. It also slips undetected into a Green Goddess dressing, blue cheese dressing, or horseradish cream. You can use tofu by itself to make a dairy- and egg-free salad dressing, but if you're a little nervous about going solo with tofu, you can successfully cut it with sour cream or yogurt, or simply add some pureed tofu to a recipe you've already made, perhaps increasing the seasonings a bit.

Spinach and Sesame Tofu Salad with Pickled Ginger

SERVES 4

This salad works well as a first course, for it is mustardy and strong. The spinach, when cooked, becomes rather concentrated. In addition to making this salad as shown here, you can go on to some interesting variations, which are described at the end of the recipe.

1 bunch (about 1 pound) spinach

Salt

1/2 carton soft tofu or 1 aseptic box firm silken tofu

2 tablespoons black and/or white sesame seeds

•

The Dressing

2 teaspoons dry mustard

1 tablespoon water

4 teaspoons dark sesame oil

2 tablespoons soy sauce

4 teaspoons rice wine vinegar

1 tablespoon sherry or rice wine

1/2 teaspoon salt

1 teaspoon finely chopped ginger

1/2 teaspoon finely chopped garlic

1 teaspoon sugar

1 heaping tablespoon slivered, pickled ginger

1. Fill a wide skillet with water and bring to a boil. Wash the spinach well, discarding the stems and any yellow or bruised leaves. Retrieve 8 of the crowns (the stems that are joined at the roots) and wash them, too. Cut the tofu into small cubes.

2. When the water boils, add 1/2 teaspoon salt and the spinach. Cook just until wilted, turning it a few times with a pair of tongs, then lift the spinach into a strainer and rinse under cool water. Set aside. Add the crowns to the pan, cook for about 15 seconds, then remove and rinse. Turn off the heat and slide the tofu into the water. Let sit for 1 minute, then carefully remove onto paper toweling to dry.

3. Roast the sesame seeds in a small dry skillet until fragrant, then remove to a plate. Combine the dressing ingredients in a small bowl.

4. Squeeze the water out of the spinach and chop, neither too fine nor too coarse. Set in a bowl and toss with 3 tablespoons of the dressing and about two thirds of the sesame seeds. Taste and add more dressing, if desired. Distribute the spinach among 4 small plates, then place the tofu around and on top. Spoon more dressing over the tofu (you probably won't use it all), then garnish with the slivered, pickled ginger and remaining sesame seeds. Place 2 spinach crowns on each plate and serve.

Wilted Spinach Salad: Heat all but 4 teaspoons of the dressing until sizzling, then pour it, while tossing, over very tender spinach leaves to wilt them. Add most of the sesame seeds and toss again. Divide among 4 plates; place the tofu among the leaves and drizzle with the remaining dressing. Add the ginger, and sprinkle the remaining sesame seeds over the top.

Green and White Rice Salad: Finely chop the cooked spinach and add it along with the sesame seeds to 2 cups freshly cooked warm white rice, a finely diced cucumber, and 2 finely slivered scallions. Toss well, then add the tofu and toss *once* before serving so as not to break it up.

Chilled Soba with Soft Tofu and Soy-Sesame Sauce

MAKES 4 APPETIZERS
OR 2 TO 3 MAIN DISHES

An ideal dish for a hot day, these noodles and tofu are cool, light, and refreshing. The sauce can also be used for tofu, either cooked or raw, without the noodles. Adding a tablespoon of peanut butter or tahini makes it a little more substantial, and adding 1/2 teaspoon of chile oil makes it a little more piquant.

For tofu, I especially like the water-packed soft and silken tofu, such as that made by Azumaya.

One 8-ounce package soba (buckwheat noodles)

1 bunch slender scallions, including a few inches of the greens, thinly sliced

1 1/2 tablespoons white or black sesame seeds

1 carton fresh soft tofu or 2 boxes firm silken tofu

The Sauce:

6 tablespoons soy sauce, such as Kikkoman or thin Chinese soy sauce

2 tablespoons rice wine vinegar

1 1/2 teaspoons dark sesame oil

1 teaspoon sugar or more to taste

1 tablespoon finely minced ginger

1. Cook the noodles in boiling water until tender but still retain a bite, about 6 to 8 minutes. Drain and rinse under cold water to stop the cooking. Shake off the excess water. (If you're cooking them ahead of time, refrigerate.) Toast the sesame seeds in a dry skillet over medium heat until fragrant, then transfer to a dish and set aside. Carefully open the tofu and turn it onto a cutting board to drain while you make the sauce.

2. Combine the ingredients for the sauce in a bowl. Taste to make sure the balance is the way you like it. It may seem salty, but remember that it's going on tofu.

3. Toss the noodles with half the scallions and sesame seeds, then divide among four plates. Make a little depression in the center. Dice the tofu into 1/2 inch cubes and set them in the center of the noodles. Spoon the sauce over the tofu and the noodles, then sprinkle with the remaining scallions and sesame seeds. Serve.

The Sesame Dressing

1 tablespoon minced ginger

1 large garlic clove, chopped

1/2 large jalapeño chile, seeded and chopped (about 1 heaping tablespoon)

4 teaspoons sesame paste or tahini

1 tablespoon dark sesame oil

1 tablespoon light sesame or vegetable oil

1 tablespoon soy sauce

2 tablespoons rice wine vinegar

1/2 teaspoon white or light brown sugar, to taste

3 tablespoons chopped cilantro

1 tablespoon chopped mint

•

1 box firm silken tofu or 1 carton soft tofu, drained

Salt

6 cups thinly slivered napa cabbage

1 small cucumber, peeled, seeded, and finely diced

Handful sunflower seed sprouts or purple broccoli sprouts

1 tablespoon toasted black or white sesame seeds

Silken Tofu and Napa Cabbage with Sesame Dressing

SERVES 4

This salad looks so good when it's rather formally arranged that I think it actually tastes better. Make individual salads or one large one, but either way, toss everything before serving.

1. Puree all the dressing ingredients, except the herbs, until smooth in a small food processor or blender, then stir in the herbs.

2. Dice the tofu into pieces about the size of a sugar cube. Bring 4 cups water to a simmer in a 10- to 12-inch skillet, add 1/2 teaspoon salt, then ease the tofu into the pan. Simmer for 2 minutes, then remove. Let cool on a towel. (If you're using water-packed soft tofu, you may prefer not to cook it. Just let the block drain on toweling while you prepare everything else.)

3. Toss the cabbage with half the dressing, then divide among 4 plates. Arrange the tofu on top and spoon the remaining dressing over it. Garnish with the cucumber, sprouts, and sesame seeds.

Variation: Include thinly sliced radishes, kohlrabi, purple cabbage and spinach leaves, paper-thin carrot shavings, white mushrooms, fresh peas or boiled fresh soybeans (edamame).

Fresh Coriander and Peanut Salad

SERVES 4 TO 6

A veritable homage to cilantro, this amazing salad comes from Bruce Cost's Book of Asian Ingredients, a book that's unfortunately out of print. (If you're interested in understanding Asian ingredients, look for it in used book stores.) This salad should be served by itself in small portions, as it's quite intensely flavored. I also like to serve it over warm white rice garnished with additional chopped peanuts.

1 carton firm tofu, drained and pressed for deep-frying (page 12)

2 cups peanut or vegetable oil

1/2 cup raw, unsalted peanuts

2 large bunches cilantro (fresh coriander), most of the stems removed

1 1/2 tablespoons light soy sauce

1/2 teaspoon sea salt

1 teaspoon sugar

1 tablespoon dark sesame or roasted peanut oil

1. Cut the pressed tofu crosswise into 6 slabs, then into a medium dice. Wick up any extra water with a paper towel.

2. Heat the oil in a 10-inch cast-iron or other heavy skillet until nearly smoking. Add the tofu, 5 or 6 pieces at a time, and fry until golden. You may have to separate them as they cook since they tend to gravitate toward each other. Set on paper towels to drain off the extra oil, then place in a bowl.

3. Drop the peanuts into the hot oil and turn off the heat. Let them sit until they turn golden, after a few minutes, then remove and set on paper towels to drain.

4. Bring a quart of water to a boil. Add the cilantro, give it a stir, then drain it into a colander. Rinse under cold running water, then squeeze out the excess moisture. Chop finely.

5. Add the peanuts and chopped cilantro to the tofu along with the remaining ingredients. Toss well, then serve.

Peppered Tofu Crisps (page 30)

The Dressing

3 tablespoons balsamic vinegar

2 tablespoons rice wine vinegar

3 tablespoons light soy sauce

2 tablespoons dark sesame oil

1 tablespoon light sesame or peanut oil

1 teaspoon dark miso

1 teaspoon dry mustard

1 teaspoon brown sugar

1/8 teaspoon salt

1 small red onion, thinly sliced

1 large yellow bell pepper, sliced about
   1/4 inch thick

5 cups thinly sliced red cabbage

1 to 2 cups snow peas, stems and strings
   removed

1 cup fresh or frozen peas

2 scallions, including some of the
   greens, thinly sliced into rounds

3 tablespoons chopped cilantro

1 tablespoon toasted black sesame
   seeds

Warm Red Cabbage Salad with Peppered Tofu Crisps

SERVES 4

Darkly glazed peppered tofu crisps are hidden in this warm salad. Although this is a cooked salad, it should be served right away; it tastes best warm, plus its colors grow dingy if it sits around.

1. Make the peppered tofu crisps and set them aside.

2. Whisk the dressing ingredients together, making sure the miso is completely blended.

3. Heat one-fourth of the dressing in a wide skillet over high heat. Add the onion and yellow pepper and cook briskly, stirring often until softened, about 4 minutes. Remove to a plate. Return the skillet to the heat and add the cabbage. Drizzle over about two-thirds of the remaining dressing and cook, turning frequently, until the cabbage has softened but still retains its bright color, about 4 minutes. Add the snow peas and pod peas, fresh or frozen, during the last minute and turn off the heat.

4. Heat the remaining dressing in a small skillet. Add the tofu and turn briskly in the dressing until glazed. It will be quite dark. Add it to the cabbage and toss a few times to mix it in.

5. Mound the cabbage and tofu on a large plate, garnish with the peppers, onions, scallions, cilantro, and sesame seeds. Serve.

Poached Salmon and Potato Salad with Fresh Herb Sauce

SERVES 4

The tofu is hidden in the sauce, and even friends of mine who approach tofu with firm suspicion never guessed it was there. This herb-laced sauce is not only perfect for the chilled salmon and steamed potatoes, but it's friendly with a host of other dishes, such as a dressing for romaine salads, vegetable slaws, warm flageolet beans, and green beans. You can take it right through the season of your herb garden, replacing the dill with marjoram, lovage, chervil, tarragon, and lemon thyme.

One 12 to 16 ounce salmon fillet, skin on
Salt
1 pound fingerling or other potatoes

The Sauce
1/2 box silken tofu or 6 ounces soft tofu
1/2 cup yogurt
2 tablespoons sour cream or mayonnaise
1 tablespoon extra virgin olive oil
2 teaspoons finely grated lemon zest, plus 1 tablespoon lemon juice
1/3 cup finely chopped fresh dill
2 garlic cloves, coarsely chopped
2 tablespoons finely snipped chives plus blossoms, if available
Pinch salt and freshly ground white pepper
1 bunch watercress, washed and trimmed

1. Rinse off the salmon, then place it in a pan, cover with cold water, and add a heaping tablespoon of salt. Bring the water to a boil, then turn off the heat and let stand for 25 minutes. Lift the salmon out, remove the skin, and refrigerate, covered, until ready to use.

2. Closer to serving time, scrub the potatoes, cut them in half (lengthwise if fingerlings), and steam over boiling water until tender when pierced with a knife, about 20 minutes.

3. Puree the tofu in a food processor with the yogurt, sour cream, and olive oil until perfectly smooth. Add lemon zest, lemon juice to taste, dill, and garlic, and process again until smooth and pale green.

4. Scrape into a bowl and stir in all but a few of the chives. Taste for salt and season with pepper. Wipe the bowl so that it looks neat, sprinkle over the remaining chives and chive blossoms. Chill until ready to use.

5. To serve, flake the salmon onto 4 plates, add the potatoes and watercress. Spoon a little sauce over the salad and garnish with chives.

1 carton soft or firm tofu, drained

Sea salt and freshly ground black pepper

1/2 cup mayonnaise

Finely grated zest and juice of
    1 large lime

3 tablespoons chopped cilantro

1/4 cup finely chopped parsley

1 teaspoon curry powder

2 scallions, thinly sliced

1 celery rib, finely diced

1 tablespoon mango chutney

Curried "Chicken" Salad

MAKES ABOUT 2 1/2 CUPS

1. Cut the tofu into cubes or strips about 1/3 inch across. Bring 6 cups water to a boil, add 1 teaspoon salt, and turn off the heat. Lower the tofu into the water and let it sit for 2 minutes. Gently tip it into a wide colander, then rinse under cool water. Shake off the excess moisture and turn the tofu onto a clean kitchen towel to dry.

2. Combine the remaining ingredients. Taste and adjust the seasonings, adding more curry powder or lime juice, if needed, to make it a little more zesty. Add the tofu and gently toss with a rubber spatula. If possible, chill 20 minutes or more. The flavors will emerge and mellow as the salad stands.

Serve this curried tofu in butter-lettuce leaves garnished with roasted cashews or chunks of chutney, or as a sandwich filling. Steeping the tofu in hot water firms up the texture and rounds out the flavor. The directions call for rather large pieces, but if you prefer, break up the tofu with a fork.

Tofu Salad Sandwich Filling

MAKES

Tofu "egg" salad has been around at least since the seventies. The texture is fine; what it needs is plenty of seasonings. Fresh herbs, especially marjoram and lovage, should you have some in your garden, are ideal. Unless you're avoiding eggs, there's no reason why you can't add one or more to the salad.

Sandwich the salad between the bread of your choice— white, wheat, or an interesting herb or olive bread—with several peppery watercress or arugula leaves.

1 carton firm tofu

1 or 2 hard-boiled eggs, mashed (optional)

¹/₄ cup finely diced celery

¹/₄ cup finely diced white onion or scallion

¹/₄ cup finely chopped parsley

3 tablespoons chopped marjoram, dill, or tarragon

2 lovage leaves, minced

¹/₃ cup mayonnaise

2 teaspoons mustard

2 tablespoons capers, rinsed

1 teaspoon paprika

¹/₄ teaspoon turmeric

Dash lemon juice or white wine vinegar

Salt and freshly ground black pepper

1. Drain the tofu, place it in a clean kitchen towel, grab the corners, and twist firmly to force out the water so that it won't dilute the dressing. Put the tofu in a bowl with the eggs, if using.

2. Add the remaining ingredients and work together with a fork. Taste and adjust the seasonings, if necessary, so that they're bright and lively.

1 carton firm tofu

$1/2$ cup fresh oregano

2 garlic cloves

12 almonds or 2 tablespoons pine nuts

3 tablespoons olive oil, plus oil for the
pan

Salt and pepper

1 cup grated Parmesan cheese

$1/2$ cup fresh bread crumbs

*Fresh oregano, garlic, almonds,
and Parmesan make a lively
coating for fried tofu. Delicious
in a sandwich with thick slices
of ripe, juicy tomatoes.*

1. Drain the tofu, slice it crosswise into 6 pieces, then set on paper toweling to drain.

2. Coarsely chop the oregano, garlic, and nuts, then put them in a mortar or small food processor with $1/2$ teaspoon salt and $1/4$ teaspoon pepper. Pound or process to make a paste, then add the 3 tablespoons olive oil.

3. Remove the tofu from the towels, season lightly with salt, then rub the pesto onto both sides. Combine the cheese and bread crumbs, then press them into the tofu.

4. Heat a nonstick or cast-iron skillet and coat generously with olive or vegetable oil. When hot, add the tofu. Fry on both sides over medium heat until golden and crisp.

Bachelor Tofu Sandwiches

MAKES 4

In about 15 minutes you can go from looking at a carton of tofu to sitting down to a savory hot sandwich. What's inside it? Sautéed onions and mushrooms covering golden tofu glazed with Worcestershire sauce or A-1 sauce, if you prefer.

1 carton firm tofu, drained
2 teaspoons olive oil
2 to 3 tablespoons Worcestershire sauce
Salt and freshly ground black pepper
1 large red or yellow onion, cut into
 ¼-inch slices

4 big mushrooms, sliced as thick
 as the onions
8 slices bread
Mustard and horseradish

1. Slice the tofu crosswise into 8 pieces, slightly less than ½ inch thick. Set them on paper towels and blot. Don't worry about the tofu getting really dry. It will dry as it cooks.

2. Heat a large cast-iron skillet. Brush with 2 teaspoons of the oil and add the tofu. Cook over medium-high heat until golden, about 6 minutes on each side. Douse with the Worcestershire sauce and turn the tofu once. Continue frying until the sauce is absorbed and the tofu is laced with a fine glaze. Turn off the heat and season well with salt and plenty of pepper.

3. While the tofu is cooking, place a 10-inch skillet over high heat and add the remaining oil. Add the onion and mushrooms. Sauté until seared and nicely browned, 5 to 7 minutes. Season with salt and pepper.

4. Toast the bread or not, as you wish. Cover with mustard and horseradish (fresh tomatoes and mayonnaise would be good here as well), add the tofu slices, top with the onions, close, press, and dig in.

One 10-ounce package falafel mix, about
    2 cups if you buy it in bulk
1 box silken tofu, soft or firm, or 1 cup
    regular soft tofu

3/4 cup water
Olive oil, for frying

MAKES TWELVE 3-INCH PATTIES

1. Place the falafel mix into a bowl.

2. Puree the tofu with the water in a food processor until smooth, then stir it into the falafel. Let it rest at least 15 minutes.

3. Film a cast-iron or nonstick skillet generously with olive oil. Divide the batter in half, then each half into sixths; doing this by eye is fine. Shape into patties about 3/8 inch thick, cook over medium heat until browned. Turn and cook the second side until browned. Serve right away. ●

Here's an instance where you won't know there's any tofu present. I shape the falafel patties a little more thinly than usual so that any extra moisture from the tofu cooks off. Eat these as you would any other falafel—in a pita sandwich, on a plate with a salad, with yogurt and tahini, or the Yogurt Sauce with Cayenne and Dill on page 48.

Curried Tofu Crumble in Pita Bread

MAKES ABOUT 3 CUPS, ENOUGH FOR 3 SANDWICHES

Full of big flavors, quick and easy to assemble, this is based on an Indian recipe called paneer bhurjee. Serve with chapatis or tucked into whole wheat pita bread with a dollop of chutney and thick yogurt—an unusual and very good sandwich.

1 carton firm tofu, pressed
1/2 teaspoon turmeric
Juice of 1/2 lime
Salt
2 tablespoons vegetable oil
1 heaping tablespoon chopped ginger
1 jalapeño chile or 1 serrano chile, seeded and minced

1 heaping tablespoon chopped garlic
1 1/2 teaspoons crushed cumin seeds
2 onions, finely diced
1/4 teaspoon cayenne pepper
2 Roma tomatoes, seeded and diced
3 tablespoons chopped cilantro
1/2 teaspoon masala (optional)

1. Crumble the tofu onto a cloth towel, then gather the ends and twist firmly to get rid of any excess moisture. The tofu should be fairly dry for this dish. Turn it into a bowl and toss with half the turmeric, the lime juice, and a few pinches of salt. Set aside while you prepare the rest of the ingredients.

2. Heat the oil in a sauté pan and add the ginger, chile, and garlic. Sauté over medium-high heat for 2 minutes or less, if the garlic begins to color. Add the cumin, onions, remaining turmeric, and cayenne and cook, stirring occasionally, until the onions are soft, about 5 minutes.

3. Add the tomatoes and raise the heat, stirring and cooking until the juices have disappeared, then lower the heat and add the tofu. Season the dish with 1/2 teaspoon salt or more to taste, and cook until the tofu is heated through, 3 to 5 minutes. Stir in the cilantro, sprinkle with the masala, if using, and turn into a serving dish. Serve hot or at room temperature.

1 carton firm tofu, pressed

1 tablespoon olive oil

1 large onion, finely diced

2 1/2 teaspoons dried or 4 tablespoons fresh marjoram

1/2 teaspoon dried or 1 1/2 teaspoons fresh thyme

8 ounces mushrooms, finely chopped (about 3 cups)

2 teaspoons Worcestershire sauce

1 to 2 tablespoons mushroom soy sauce or tamari

2 large garlic cloves, minced or squeezed through a press

1 1/2 teaspoons Dijon mustard

1 cup roasted walnuts or cashews, finely ground

1 cup bread crumbs

Salt and freshly ground black pepper

1 egg

Tofu-Walnut Croquettes on English Muffins

MAKES 6 LARGE CAKES

These are light and almost fluffy, but if you prefer a denser texture, use cooked brown rice or bulgur in place of the bread crumbs. Begin by pressing the tofu to eliminate the excess moisture. Serve the croquettes on English muffins with mustard and a little mayonnaise.

1. Wrap the tofu in a clean dish towel and place it on a cutting board that's tilted toward the sink. Place a heavy object on top and set aside to drain while you prepare everything else.

2. Heat the oil in a wide nonstick skillet. Add the onion, marjoram, and thyme. Cover and cook over medium-high heat, stirring frequently, for 5 minutes. Add the mushrooms and cook over high heat, stirring more frequently, until the mushrooms have reabsorbed any liquid, about 8 minutes. Add the Worcestershire sauce, soy sauce, and garlic. Stir rapidly for a minute. If the garlic begins to darken, remove the pan from the heat. Scrape the onion-mushroom mixture into a bowl. Add the ground nuts, bread crumbs, and mustard.

3. Crumble the tofu into the skillet. Sauté over high heat, stirring frequently, until lightly colored but still tender to the touch. Season it with salt and pepper, then add it to the onion mixture. Taste. You may need to add more salt, pepper, mustard, and/or soy sauce before you add the egg.

4. Add the egg. Divide the mixture into 1/2 cup portions and shape into rounds or ovals. Lightly brush a nonstick skillet with olive oil, then fry the croquettes until golden, carefully turning them once with a spatula.

Yogurt Sauce with Cayenne and Dill

MAKES 1¹/₂ CUPS

This is my universal sauce because it can go everywhere and with everything. For years I've made it with 1 cup drained yogurt and half as much sour cream, but with such robust seasonings as garlic, cayenne, and dill, tofu can fit into the mix quite easily whether you're using tofu alone or tofu mixed with yogurt and sour cream.

1 cup silken tofu

¹/₂ cup drained yogurt- or sour cream (or additional tofu)

2 tablespoons extra-virgin olive oil, plus extra for garnish

1 large garlic clove

¹/₂ teaspoon salt

2 tablespoons chopped fresh dill

¹/₄ teaspoon cayenne pepper or hot paprika

1. Puree the tofu in a food processor with the yogurt and oil until perfectly smooth, stopping to scrape down the sides of the bowl.

2. In a mortar, mash the garlic with the salt until smooth, then add it to tofu-yogurt mixture along with the dill and cayenne. Scrape into a serving bowl and refrigerate for an hour so that the garlic-dill-cayenne mixture will suffuse the sauce with its flavor. Just before serving, garnish with a swirl of additional oil and a pinch of cayenne or paprika.

Variations: In place of dill, use a mixture of chopped dill, basil, parsley, and mint. Or, if you're a fan of fresh coriander, replace the dill with finely chopped cilantro. Watercress and chives are another, more peppery combination.

1/2 cup tofu or regular mayonnaise

2 teaspoons tamari

1 garlic clove, minced

1 small shallot, finely diced

1 tablespoon chopped parsley

Freshly ground white pepper

Mix everything in a small bowl and season with pepper to taste.

Tamari Mayonnaise

MAKES ABOUT 1/2 CUP

A simple mayonnaise is made unique by adding tamari. It's a good sauce to use on simply prepared tofu dishes, like the Bachelor Tofu Sandwiches on page 44, the Oregano Crusted Tofu on page 43, or grilled tofu.

1/2 box silken tofu or 6 ounces soft tofu

2 to 4 tablespoons olive oil

2 tablespoons mayonnaise

2 garlic cloves, coarsely chopped

1 1/2 cups coarsely chopped cilantro, large stems removed

1 teaspoon sugar

Grated zest and juice of 2 limes

Salt

1. Puree the tofu with the olive oil and mayonnaise in a small food processor until smooth. Scrape down the sides and puree again.

2. Add the garlic, cilantro, sugar, lime zest, half the lime juice, and 1/2 teaspoon salt. Puree until smooth and green. Taste for salt and lime juice, adding more, if needed. Scrape into a bowl and chill until ready to use.

Cilantro-Lime Mayonnaise

MAKES ABOUT 1 CUP

Use this mayonnaise to bind a chicken salad, a tuna salad, or a Waldorf-type salad of apples, celery, jicama, and pine nuts.

Tofu Mayonnaise

MAKES ABOUT 1 CUP

Here's an all-tofu mayonnaise, but your family may never suspect, especially if you add a tablespoon or more of prepared mayonnaise—a good idea if you're nervous about it. This will keep, refrigerated, for up to five days.

6 ounces soft tofu, well drained, or $1/2$ box silken tofu

2 tablespoons prepared mayonnaise (optional)

$1/3$ cup olive oil

1 small garlic clove

2 teaspoons Dijon mustard

$2 1/2$ teaspoons fresh lemon juice or vinegar (red or white wine)

Salt and freshly ground white pepper

1. Put the tofu in a food processor with the mayonnaise, if using, and oil. Puree until smooth. Scrape down the sides.

2. Add the garlic, mustard, lemon juice, and $1/4$ teaspoon salt, and puree until smooth. Taste for salt and season with a little pepper. Scrape into a bowl and refrigerate until ready to use.

Mustard Mayonnaise: Increase the mustard to 4 to 5 teaspoons, or to taste.

Garlic Mayonnaise: Coarsely chop 4 to 6 cloves unblemished garlic. Pound in a mortar with 1/2 teaspoon salt until the garlic breaks down into a smooth puree, then stir it into the mayonnaise.

Saffron Mayonnaise: In a small mortar, grind 2 pinches saffron threads, then cover with 1 tablespoon boiling water. Let steep several minutes, then stir it into the mayonnaise.

Roasted Pepper Mayonnaise: Puree 1/2 cup roasted peppers until smooth with 1 garlic clove and a pinch of cayenne and add it to the mayonnaise.

Mayonnaise with Capers and Fines Herbes: Stir into the mayonnaise 2 tablespoons rinsed capers, 1/4 cup chopped parsley, 2 tablespoons each chopped tarragon and snipped chives.

Chipotle Mayonnaise: Add 1 teaspoon pureed chipotle in adobo sauce into the mayonnaise. Taste and add more if you prefer it hotter. In place of lemon in the mayonnaise, use fresh lime juice.

Coriander-Sesame Dressing

MAKES 1 CUP

4 ounces silken tofu or soft tofu, well drained

1/2 jalapeño chile, seeded and chopped

Zest and juice of 1 large lime

3 tablespoons sour cream

1/2 teaspoon roasted sesame oil

1/2 cup chopped fresh coriander (cilantro) leaves

1 scallion, including an inch of the green, sliced

Salt and freshly ground white pepper

2 teaspoons snipped chives

If you're a cilantro lover, you could find yourself using this versatile recipe as a dressing, dip, or sauce—on sandwiches; spread over seared tofu or grilled fish; definitely with grilled, roasted, and steamed vegetables, such as sweet potatoes, eggplant, or asparagus. It works amazingly well as a dip for vegetables or a spread for sesame crackers. Toss it with slivered cabbage for an unusual slaw. It will keep, refrigerated, for about 1 week.

Combine the tofu, chile, lime zest and juice, sour cream, and oil in a small food processor, and puree until completely smooth, stopping several times to scrape down the sides. Add the cilantro and scallion, and puree just enough to make a flecked, pale green sauce. Season to taste with salt and pepper. Scrape into a serving bowl and sprinkle with the chives.

1 heaping tablespoon chopped ginger

1 tablespoon diced, seeded jalapeño
    chile

1 garlic clove

1/4 cup chopped cilantro

1 tablespoon tahini or sesame paste

1 teaspoon dark sesame oil

3 tablespoons fresh lime juice

4 ounces silken tofu

Salt and freshly ground white pepper

1. Put everything but the tofu in the small bowl of a food processor and process until fairly well blended, about 2 minutes.

2. Add the tofu, 1/4 teaspoon salt, and continue processing, stopping once or twice to scrape down the sides, until you have a smooth, green-flecked sauce. Taste for salt and season with pepper. If the sauce is too thick for your purposes, or if it thickens in the refrigerator, thin it by whisking in water as needed.

The texture of a thin mayonnaise, this sauce can be drizzled over cubes of soft fresh tofu, as a dressing for a romaine salad or cole slaw, or spooned over grilled fish or chicken. It also gives sautéed vegetables a finish that's as good as it is unexpected.

Horseradish Cream

MAKES ABOUT 1 CUP

If you prefer, you can use all tofu in this and the next recipe, and omit the sour cream.

$\frac{1}{2}$ cup silken or soft tofu, drained

$\frac{1}{4}$ cup sour cream

$\frac{1}{4}$ cup prepared horseradish

2 tablespoons white wine vinegar

Salt

Puree the tofu in a small food processor with the sour cream until perfectly smooth, scraping down the sides once or twice as necessary. Scrape into a bowl, stir in the horseradish, vinegar, and salt to taste.

Mustard Cream

MAKES ABOUT 1 CUP

The character of this sauce depends mainly on the mustard you use, from scary ballpark mustard to grainy German to smooth Dijon, or a sweet honey mustard. Use your favorite.

3/4 cup silken or soft tofu, drained

$\frac{1}{4}$ cup sour cream

4 teaspoons mustard, or more to taste

1 small shallot or white onion, finely diced

Salt and freshly ground black pepper

Puree the tofu and sour cream until smooth, then stir in the mustard and shallot, and season with salt and pepper to taste.

MISO SOUP, THE FIRST DISH TO ARRIVE at the table in a Japanese restaurant, often comes with tiny cubes of silken tofu, so for many, tofu in soup is already a familiar sight. Here, I've included both traditional and new ways of using tofu in this sampler of soups. While I don't think it necessarily makes sense to add diced tofu to every soup, in general it does work well in brothy soups seasoned with ginger, soy, lemongrass, coconut milk and other Asian seasonings.

If you wish to incorporate tofu into thicker soups, you're better off adding it as a puree. For example, the first time I made the peanut soup on page 62 I sautéed the tofu with paprika for color and flavor, but the paprika dissolved, leaving the tofu looking pale, out of place, and frankly unappealing. The second time I pureed the tofu with a portion of the soup, then added it back in, where it disappeared without a trace.

Using this method, you can include tofu in virtually any soup that's going to be pureed entirely or in part, but it won't be obvious. Always, when pureed tofu is to be cooked, make sure it's perfectly smooth before adding it to the soup, so you don't end up with little gobbets of tofu. You can use any kind of tofu for this, but the softer it is, the easier it will be to achieve silky smoothness.

At the end of this chapter, you will find three vegetable stocks.

Miso Soup with Silken Tofu

SERVES 4

Although all kinds of garnishes can go into a miso soup, rest assured that tofu is always welcome. If you've made the stock, include the mushroom caps, thinly sliced, in the soup.

5 cups Mushroom-Kombu Stock (page 64), daishi no moto, or water
1 carton soft tofu, drained, or 1 box silken tofu
3 fresh shiitake, stems discarded, or white mushrooms
4 tablespoons dark or white miso, or more to taste
Soy sauce (optional)
2 scallions, including the greens, thinly sliced on the diagonal
Few drops chili oil

1. Bring the stock to a simmer. Dice the tofu into ¼- to ½-inch cubes and thinly slice the mushrooms.

2. Remove 1 cup of the stock and work it into the miso until you have a smooth paste. Add the tofu and shiitakes to the pot. About the time the stock returns to a boil, the tofu will be nearly heated through.

3. Add the diluted miso to the pot and turn off the heat. Taste for strength, adding more miso or soy sauce, if desired. Serve in bowls, add the scallions and a few drops of chili oil to each.

Miso Soup with Spinach Crowns: While the stock is simmering, trim the root ends of the spinach, or crowns, as they're called. The crowns are the base of the plant and are usually thrown away. Rinse them well, set in a bowl of cold water to soak for 15 minutes, in order to loosen any sand, then rinse them again. Add them to the soup with the tofu. They should just have wilted to tenderness by the time the tofu is heated through.

4 teaspoons olive or sesame oil

1 small onion, diced

1 carrot, peeled and diced

1 celery rib, diced

3 red bell peppers, veins and seeds
  removed, chopped

1 teaspoon chopped fresh thyme

3 tablespoons chopped parsley

Salt

2 tablespoons dark miso

5 cups water, chicken stock, or Basic
  Vegetable Stock (page 63)

1 tablespoon dark soy sauce

Garnish

4 ounces firm silken tofu, finely diced

1 heaping tablespoon black sesame
  seeds

1 tablespoon snipped chives

Miso tempers the sweetness of red bell peppers and tones their color down to a burnished red-orange. This smooth soup is garnished with tiny cubes of soft tofu that have been simmered in salted water, a scattering of black sesame seeds, and snipped chives.

1. Heat the oil in a wide soup pot. Add the onion, carrot, celery, bell peppers, and herbs. Sauté over high heat, stirring frequently, until the vegetables are wilted, browned in places, and there's a dark film on the bottom of the pot. Add 1 teaspoon salt and stir in the miso.

2. Add 1 cup of the water and scrape the pan to release the juices and break up the miso. Add the remaining water and soy sauce, bring to a boil, then lower the heat and cover the pan. Simmer for 25 minutes. Let cool briefly.

3. Puree the soup until smooth, then pass through a sieve or food mill to get rid of the pepper skins.

4. Bring 1 quart water to boil in a skillet or small sauce pan. Add 1 teaspoon salt, then reduce the heat so that the water is barely simmering. Add the tofu, simmer for 2 minutes, then remove. Heat the sesame seeds in a dry skillet until they smell toasty, then remove to a plate.

5. Serve the soup in individual bowls, add tofu to each, and sprinkle with the sesame seeds and chives. If you have any chive blossoms, scatter a few in each bowl.

About Miso Soups

Miso, made from fermented soy beans, makes a quick, invigorating soup. If you're feeling a little under the weather, you may well find this soup doubly comforting. Miso soup is perfect for using the more delicate silken and soft tofus. Handle them gently, carrying them on the edge of a vegetable knife or spatula to the soup so they don't break. When added to the soup, the tofu will sink, but as it heats through, it will rise to the surface.

Misos vary a great deal in intensity and flavor. A true, aged Hatcho miso is dark and rich, while lighter misos are more delicate and sweet. Some include barley, others are seasoned with ginger, which means you'll just have to taste as you go, adding more miso or soy sauce or tamari, if needed.

For most everyday soups, a dark miso seems to be most popular. The vegetable garnishes are many. *Wakame* seaweed, sliced mushrooms, little spinach leaves, slivered carrots and asparagus, snow peas, and even avocado. If the vegetables you've chosen need time to become tender, cook them separately and add them at the end.

As for broth, you can really do quite well using water, which is one of the blessings of miso soup. Or you can introduce more depth by making a simple stock based on kombu, a kind of sea green, or by using daishi no moto, the Japanese stock based on dried bonito, a tunalike fish. The latter can be found in powdered form in Japanese stores and many natural food stores.

4 to 5 cups Vegetable Stock for Asian
   Dishes (page 64)
4 ounces thin somen (Japanese
   noodles) or linguine
1 bunch bok choy
1 tablespoon peanut oil
1 tablespoon finely chopped ginger
1 teaspoon finely chopped garlic
1/2 cup chopped cilantro leaves

Soy sauce, to taste
1 carton soft tofu, drained, or 1 box firm
   silken tofu, diced into small cubes
4 to 6 fresh shiitake (or other)
   mushrooms, stems discarded,
   caps thinly sliced
1/2 teaspoon red chili oil, or more to taste
8 cilantro sprigs, for garnish

The tofu simmers in the broth, the bok choy and noodles are stir-fried, then all are brought together to make this invigorating soup. This dish can be a main course for two, or part of a meal for four. The dried mushrooms flavor the stock, then are slivered and used in the soup.

1. First make the vegetable stock. Reserve the dried mushrooms from the stock, discard the stems, and thinly slice the caps. Strain the stock and return to the burner. Keep warm on low heat.

2. While the stock is cooking, bring several quarts of water to a boil, add the somen and cook until tender-firm, usually just 3 to 4 minutes, as they are very thin. Drain, rinse under cold water, and set aside. Slice the whites and greens of the bok choy diagonally about 1/2 inch thick, then wash.

3. When you're ready to eat, heat a wok or large skillet and add the oil. When it's hot, add the ginger, garlic, cilantro, and bok choy, and stir-fry for 1 minute. Add 1/2 cup of the stock. Cook until the bok choy has begun to brighten in color, another minute. Add the somen, 1 tablespoon soy sauce, and heat through.

4. Add the tofu and all the mushrooms to the remaining stock.

5. When the noodles are hot and the bok choy is cooked, divide them among 4 bowls. Divide the tofu as well, then spoon over the broth. Add a few drops of chili oil to each bowl then garnish with the cilantro sprigs. Serve with extra soy sauce and chili oil on the side.

Clear Soup with Sweet Potatoes, Silken Tofu, and Mustard Greens

SERVES 4

This is a light and nourishing soup. It's a nice touch to use two kinds of sweet potatoes; try a deep red Garnet yam and a lighter Jewel, for color contrast. Use silken tofu or a carton of soft tofu, but drain it well so it doesn't thin the soup.

The Broth

2 teaspoons vegetable oil

2 teaspoons dark sesame oil

1 heaping tablespoon coarsely chopped garlic

1 heaping tablespoon chopped ginger

1 large jalapeño chile, diced, seeds left in for more heat

1/4 cup thinly sliced cilantro stems

6 cups chicken stock, water, or Vegetable Stock for Asian Dishes (page 64)

Pinch five-spice powder

1 teaspoon salt

About 12 ounces sweet potatoes, peeled and diced into 1/2-inch chunks (2 cups)

3 cups mustard greens, stems discarded, leaves cut into ribbons

1 box silken tofu, cubed, or 1 carton soft tofu, drained and cubed

2 scallions, including the greens, sliced diagonally about 1/4 inch wide

Few drops soy or mushroom soy sauce per bowl, if needed

1. Heat the vegetable oil and half the sesame oil in a soup pot. When hot, add the garlic, ginger, chile, and cilantro, and stir-fry for 2 minutes. Add the stock, five-spice powder, and salt. Bring to a boil, then lower the heat, and simmer, covered, for 15 minutes. Strain and return to the pan, or simply lift out the chopped flavorings with a small skimmer. Press out as much liquid as you can, then discard.

2. Add the sweet potatoes to the pot and simmer, covered, for 10 minutes, or until tender when pierced with a knife.

3. Add the greens and tofu. Cook gently, uncovered, until the greens are bright green and tender and the tofu is hot, about 5 minutes. Add the scallions. Taste for salt and add the remaining sesame oil. Add the soy sauce, by drops, to taste, if the dish seems to need a little extra punch. Ladle the soup into bowls and serve.

1 small butternut squash

4 teaspoons roasted peanut oil

1 cup minced onion

2 garlic cloves, minced

4 pieces galangal or slices fresh ginger

Grated zest and juice of 1 large lime

1/4 teaspoon turmeric

1 to 2 teaspoons Thai red chili paste

4 cups chicken stock or Basic Vegetable
   Stock (page 63)

Sea salt

1/4 cup chopped cilantro leaves

2 tablespoons basil leaves, thinly sliced

One can coconut milk

One 10-ounce box silken tofu or 1 carton
   soft tofu, drained

Coconut–Red Curry Soup with Butternut Squash and Lime

SERVES 4 TO 6

Rich, succulent, silky, and hot are words that come to mind for this soup. Its intensity makes it ideal for a first course, but an entire meal of it will certainly be sufficiently filling and act as a corrective for sniffles and allergies.

1. Peel the squash with a vegetable peeler, halve and scoop out the seeds, then dice into 1/2-inch cubes. You should have 3 to 4 cups. (If you're making a vegetable stock, add the skins and seeds from the squash to the stock.)

2. Warm the oil in a wide soup pot. Add the onion, squash, garlic, galangal, lime zest, and turmeric. Cook over medium-high heat, stirring frequently, for about 5 minutes, then add the chili paste.

3. Add 1/2 cup water and scrape the pot to dilute the paste, then add the stock and 1/2 teaspoon salt. Bring to a boil, then reduce the heat to low, cover the pot, and simmer for 20 minutes. Meanwhile, dice the tofu into small cubes and prepare the cilantro and basil.

4. Add the coconut milk to the soup, followed by the tofu. Simmer until the soup is hot again and the tofu is heated through, about 5 minutes. Taste for salt, adding more if necessary. Add the cilantro and basil, and squeeze in the juice from the lime. Serve immediately. (If you plan to serve the soup long after making it, add the cilantro, basil, and lime when you reheat it.)

Peanut Soup with Rice and Scallions

SERVES 6

Instead of white cubes of tofu bobbing in this African-style, soup where they look decidedly odd, I puree the tofu with a portion of the finished soup until everything is smooth. The tofu is there, but it doesn't intrude. And this is a method you can use with virtually any pureed soup.

If you wish, you can puree the entire soup, or leave it textured, with bits of sweet potatoes and peppers.

2 tablespoons roasted peanut or vegetable oil

2 large onions, diced

2 large bell peppers, 1 red and 1 green, diced into 1/2-inch chunks

2 teaspoons chopped ginger

2 sweet potatoes, peeled and cut into 1-inch chunks

3 large garlic cloves, finely chopped

Salt and freshly ground black pepper

1/4 teaspoon cayenne pepper or red pepper flakes, or more to taste

2 cups crushed tomatoes in sauce

5 cups water, or chicken stock, or Basic Vegetable Stock (page 63)

3/4 cup peanut butter

1 box or 1/2 carton tofu, preferably soft

2 cups cooked rice

1 cup sliced scallions, including the firm greens

1. Warm the oil in a wide soup pot set over high heat. Add the onions, bell peppers, ginger, and sweet potatoes, and sauté, stirring frequently, until the onions have begun to color, 8 to 10 minutes, adding the garlic after the first 5 minutes. Add 1 teaspoon salt, several good twists of the pepper mill, and the cayenne, to taste, and cook a few minutes longer.

2. Add the tomatoes and scrape the pot to lift up any brown bits from the bottom. Add the water or stock, bring to a boil, then lower the heat and simmer, covered, for 25 minutes.

3. Add the peanut butter and cook, stirring, until it has dissolved.

4. Remove 2 cups of the soup and puree with the tofu until perfectly smooth. Return this mixture to the soup. (If you wish, puree the entire soup.) Taste for salt and for the heat level, adding more cayenne if desired.

5. Serve with 1/3 cup rice mounded in each bowl and plenty of scallions scattered over the top.

1 tablespoon olive or vegetable oil

1 large onion

2 large carrots

2 celery ribs, including a few leaves

4 mushrooms

1 bunch scallions, including half of the
   greens

8 garlic cloves, smashed

1 tablespoon tomato paste

8 parsley sprigs with stems

6 thyme sprigs or $1/2$ teaspoon dried
   thyme

2 bay leaves

2 teaspoons salt

$1/2$ teaspoon peppercorns

2 quarts cold water

Scrub the vegetables and chop them roughly into 1 inch chunks. Heat the oil in a soup pot. Add the vegetables and herbs and cook over high heat 5 to 10 minutes, stirring frequently. The more color they get, the richer the flavor of the stock. Add the remaining ingredients and bring to a boil. Lower the heat and simmer, partially covered, for 45 minutes. Strain.

Basic Vegetable Stock

MAKES ABOUT 6 CUPS

This is a basic vegetable stock in which no special flavor predominates. Do, however, include any trimmings from the vegetables used in the soup or dish that you're making. For example, if you're making something with winter squash, add the skins and seeds in the stock as well. Leek trimmings, extra mushrooms, tomatoes (in summer), and the like are always welcome.

Vegetable Stock
for Asian Dishes

MAKES ABOUT 6 CUPS

5 fresh or dried shiitake mushrooms

1 bunch scallions, including the greens

1 onion or leek, thinly sliced (include the leek root, well washed)

3 large carrots, thinly sliced

1/2 cup cilantro stems and leaves

2 slices ginger

6 garlic cloves

One 6-inch piece kombu (optional)

1 tablespoon soy sauce

1 tablespoon mirin (rice wine)

1 1/2 teaspoons salt

1 teaspoon dark sesame oil

8 cups cold water

Combine all the ingredients in a pot and slowly bring to a boil. Reduce the heat to low and simmer, partially covered, for 45 minutes. Strain, pressing out the liquid from the vegetables.

Mushroom-Kombu
Stock

MAKES 4 CUPS

Use this stock as a base for miso soups or as a broth to pour over noodles and tofu.

5 cups water

One 6-inch piece kombu

4 dried shiitake mushrooms

4 scallions, including the roots and greens

1 small carrot, thinly sliced

1/4 cup soy sauce

1 teaspoon dark sesame oil

2 tablespoons mirin (rice wine)

Salt

1.   Combine the water, kombu, mushrooms, scallions, and carrot in a soup pot. Bring to a boil and simmer, partially covered, for 15 minutes. Remove the kombu and set it aside to dry. You can use it again.

2.   Add the soy sauce, sesame oil, mirin, and salt to taste. Simmer 10 minutes more. Remove the mushrooms and set aside, then strain. Taste and add more salt or soy, if needed. Discard the stems of the mushrooms and reserve the caps to use in miso soup or in another dish.

STIR-FRYING AND SAUTÉING are two methods that utilize high heat and rapid movement of the ingredients. Because tofu is so delicate, I nearly always fry, brown, or simmer it first so that it won't disintegrate during this lively cooking action. Precooking firms the proteins in the tofu, rendering it a little less prone to fall apart. And as a side benefit, when browned, the flavor of both the tofu and attendant seasonings is likely to be heightened.

Stir-fried tofu, in combination with a vegetable or several vegetables, as in the Lohans' or Buddha's feast, is a common menu item in Chinese restaurants. You've undoubtedly encountered it before and may even have a number of recipes for tofu stir-fries in your repertoire, or in cookbooks that you own. Ginger and garlic are nearly always at the base of a stir-fry, but there are other approaches to take when it comes to seasoning stir-fried or sautéed tofu. Southeast Asian ingredients, such as tamarind, lemongrass, and lime; Indian spices, such as cumin and turmeric; and Western herbs, such as parsley and marjoram, are all effective flavoring agents. This selection is intended to expand your seasoning horizons.

Sautéed Asparagus with Curried Tofu and Tomatoes

SERVES 3 OR 4

A coating of turmeric-laced curry turns the tofu from bright white to a rich, golden yellow. The tofu is also dusted with salt and sugar, then shallow-fried until it becomes crisp on the outside. The asparagus retains some of its crunch as well. Green beans, tipped and tailed, can be used in place of the asparagus.

The Tofu

1 carton firm tofu

Salt and freshly ground black pepper

$1/2$ teaspoon sugar

$1/2$ teaspoon curry powder

$1/4$ teaspoon turmeric

2 tablespoons, plus 2 teaspoons vegetable oil

4 garlic cloves, finely chopped

2 teaspoons roasted ground cumin seeds

1 onion, finely diced

$1/2$ pound slender asparagus, tough ends trimmed, cut diagonally into 3-inch lengths

Several pinches red pepper flakes

4 Roma tomatoes, seeded and chopped

3 tablespoons chopped cilantro

1. Dice the tofu into pieces about the size of a sugar cube. Simmer in 6 cups salted water for 2 minutes, then remove with a strainer and place on paper towels. Wick the surface with another paper towel, then toss the cubes with $1/2$ teaspoon salt, some pepper, the sugar, and curry powder.

2. Heat the 2 tablespoons oil in a wide skillet, add the tofu, and sauté over medium-high heat until golden, but still tender, about 10 minutes in all. Turn the tofu so that all the surfaces are colored. Remove to a plate, cover to keep warm, and return the pan to the heat and adjust the heat to medium.

3. Add the 2 teaspoons oil. When hot, add the garlic, $1 1/2$ teaspoons of the cumin, and the onion. Cook until the onion is translucent, then raise the heat to high. As soon as the pan feels hot, add the asparagus, pepper flakes, and a pinch or two of salt. Sauté just until the asparagus is bright green and tender, but not limp, about 5 minutes or so, the exact time depending on the size. Add the tomatoes and tofu, and cook about 1 minute more. Turn off the heat and add the cilantro and remaining cumin.

4. Slide everything onto a platter (use a bright blue one if you can) and serve immediately.

The Tofu

1 carton firm tofu, drained

1 teaspoon curry powder

Juice of 1 lime

Salt and freshly ground black pepper

3 tablespoons vegetable oil

1 teaspoon cumin seeds

1 large onion, cut into 1/2-inch wedges

1 green pepper, diced into large squares

1 heaping tablespoon chopped garlic

1 heaping tablespoon chopped ginger

1/2 teaspoon red pepper flakes

2 teaspoons ground coriander

1/8 teaspoon turmeric

4 Roma tomatoes, cut into chunks

3 tablespoons chopped cilantro

Golden Tofu Sauté with Peppers, Onions, and Tomatoes

SERVES 4

1. Drain the tofu, cut it into 3/4-inch cubes, and blot well with paper towels. Place the tofu in a large bowl and gently toss with the curry powder, half the lime juice, and season with salt and pepper. Set aside while you prepare the rest of the ingredients.

2. Heat 1 tablespoon of the oil in a nonstick skillet, add the tofu, and cook over medium-high heat, turning occasionally until golden on all the surfaces, about 4 minutes. Turn off the heat, add the remaining lime juice and set aside.

3. Heat the remaining oil in a large, nonstick skillet with the cumin seeds. When hot, add the onion and sauté over high heat until lightly browned and beginning to soften, 3 to 4 minutes. Add the green pepper, garlic, ginger, pepper flakes, coriander, and turmeric. Cook several minutes more, or until the peppers have softened a little. Season with 1 teaspoon salt. (Keep your eye on the garlic—you don't want it to burn. If the pan seems dangerously dry or hot, add 1/2 cup water and give the pan a swirl. Not only will this prevent burning, it will make a little sauce as well. You can continue adding water as needed.)

4. Add the tofu and tomatoes, and cook until the tofu is heated through, just a few minutes more. Add the cilantro and serve immediately.

An Indian recipe using paneer, a delicate white cheese, is the inspiration for this attractive dish. Everything is cut into large pieces to give the dish a great bold look. The tofu is drained, tossed in a dry marinade of curry powder and lime, then fried until crisp on the outside, but tender inside.

Lacquered Tofu Triangles with Green Beans and Cashews

SERVES 4

Easy, fast, and beguiling. Serve with rice or a baked sweet potato.

1 carton firm tofu
1 red bell pepper
1/4 pound green beans or thin asparagus
1/2 teaspoon Szechuan peppercorns

1 tablespoon mushroom soy sauce
3 tablespoons regular soy sauce
2 tablespoons light brown sugar

3 garlic cloves, minced or pressed
1/4 cup water or stock

5 teaspoons roasted peanut oil
5 scallions, including the firm greens, sliced diagonally into 1/2-inch pieces
1/4 cup roasted cashews

1. Drain the tofu. Cut it crosswise into slabs about 1/2 inch wide. Cut each slab in half lengthwise, then cut into triangles. Blot well with paper towels. Cut the bell pepper in half lengthwise, remove the veins and seeds, then cut each half into three long strips. Cut each strip into triangles. Tip and tail the beans and cut them into 2-inch lengths. Toast the Szechuan peppercorns in a dry skillet until aromatic, then grind to a powder and set aside.

2. Combine the next five ingredients in a small bowl and stir to dissolve the sugar.

3. Heat 1 tablespoon of the oil in a wide nonstick skillet over medium-high heat. Add the tofu and cook, without disturbing, until firm, about 5 minutes. Turn and cook the second side. The tofu should be golden, but still tender to the touch. Remove and set aside.

4. Add another teaspoon of oil to the pan and, when hot, add the green beans. Stir-fry over high heat for 2 minutes, then add the bell pepper and cook for another 5 minutes or so. Return the tofu to the pan and season with a few pinches of salt and the Szechuan peppercorns.

5. Pour in the soy-sauce mixture and cook, moving the pan back and forth rapidly to coat the tofu and peppers. Turn off the heat before it reduces completely. Top with cashews, and serve over rice.

1 large or 2 small bunches bok choy or
  other Chinese greens
1 carton soft or firm tofu, drained
1 cup Vegetable Stock for Asian Dishes
  (page 64), chicken stock, or water
2 tablespoons soy sauce

1 tablespoon oyster sauce (if vegetarian,
  omit or substitute Lan Chi Chilli Paste)
1 tablespoon roasted peanut oil
3 garlic cloves, minced
1/4 teaspoon salt
1 tablespoon cornstarch mixed with
  1 tablespoon water

This soothing dish of stir-fried greens and tender tofu simmered in broth thickened with cornstarch is one of my favorites. It's one I make often, especially when I've found some exceptionally fresh tofu in an Asian market. Soft tofu has a delicate almost quivery consistency, but firm tofu will work, too. Although the tofu feels rather dense when you drain it, it softens up considerably in the pan.

1. Cut the bok choy leaves into 3-inch pieces, the stems into 2-inch pieces. Wash well. Handling the tofu gently, cut it into 1-inch cubes or larger. Mix together the stock, soy sauce, and oyster sauce.

2. Heat a wide nonstick skillet, add the oil, and when hot, add the garlic and the bok choy. Sprinkle with salt and stir-fry over high heat for about 2 minutes until the greens are wilted. Add the stock, reduce the heat to low, then add the tofu. Cover and simmer until the tofu is heated through, 4 to 5 minutes. Add the diluted cornstarch and gently stir it into the juices without breaking the tofu. Serve over rice.

Tofu and Asparagus with Lemongrass Rub

SERVES 4

This is a delicate dish with a very slight crunch that is provided by sugar and salt. The marinade, plus a final browning in oil, help build the flavor and surface texture. The accompanying asparagus is served with a sauce made with the lemongrass paste, so be sure to cut everything as finely as possible.

1 carton firm tofu

3 tablespoons very finely minced lemongrass, from the center of 1 or 2 stalks

3 plump garlic cloves, minced

1 small shallot (or the whites of 2 large scallions), finely diced

2 tablespoons finely chopped cilantro stems

1 tablespoon minced ginger

1/4 teaspoon turmeric

1/2 jalapeño chile, seeded and chopped

1 tablespoon sugar

Salt and freshly ground black pepper

4 teaspoons roasted peanut oil, plus extra for the pan

1 pound asparagus, tough ends trimmed, peeled if thick

4 lime wedges, plus cilantro or watercress sprigs for garnish

1.   Drain the tofu, wrap it in a clean towel, and press while you prepare the rest of the ingredients.

2.   To make the paste, puree the next eight ingredients with 1/2 teaspoon salt and 2 teaspoons of the peanut oil in a small food processor. Or, even better, mash them with a pestle. If the mixture is too thick to work, add a little water as needed.

3. Unwrap the tofu and cut it crosswise into 8 pieces. Cut each piece in half, crosswise or diagonally. Put them on a large plate and spoon the paste over them. Use your fingers to gently press in the rub, turning the pieces over so that both sides are coated. Cover and refrigerate until ready to use. (This can be done the day before.)

4. Heat a wide, nonstick skillet and add a generous film of peanut oil. When hot, remove the tofu from its dish, leaving most of the rub behind. Place the tofu in the pan in a single layer and cook over medium heat until golden, 4 to 5 minutes. Turn and cook on the second side. Add a little cracked pepper and a sprinkling of salt.

5. While the tofu is cooking, simmer the asparagus in salted water until tender, then set on a towel to drain. Roll it in the remaining lemongrass rub and remaining roasted peanut oil. Season with salt and pepper to taste.

6. To serve, place the asparagus on a platter and intersperse with the tofu. Garnish with the cilantro and limes, which should be squeezed over everything.

Stir-fried Spicy Tofu and Cod with Scallions and Peanuts

SERVES 4

Vegetarians will find this dish is delicious without the fish (double the tofu, for quantity), but if you want to experience tofu in more gradual manner, try this recipe as written. In place of cod you can use another firm white fish or even shrimp, peeled and deveined.

1 carton firm tofu, drained and pressed (page 7)

1 pound fresh cod, rinsed and patted dry

Juice and zest of 1 lemon

2 garlic cloves, minced

2 teaspoons finely minced ginger

1 tablespoon sambal oelek (available in Asian groceries)

1 teaspoon ground coriander

1/2 teaspoon turmeric

2 tablespoons peanut oil

Salt

3/4 cup unsalted, roasted peanuts

1 bunch scallions, including about half of the greens, thinly sliced

4 lemon wedges

1. Cut both the tofu and cod into pieces about 1 1/2 inches long and 1/2 inch thick. Put them into separate bowls.

2. Divide the next seven ingredients between the two bowls and toss gently. Take care not to break up the tofu.

3. Heat half the oil in a wide, nonstick skillet. When hot, add the tofu and fry over medium-high heat until golden and crispy, 8 to 10 minutes. Turn so that all the surfaces have a chance to color. When done, sprinkle with salt, remove to a plate, and cover to keep warm. Return the pan to the heat.

4. Add the remaining oil, add the peanuts and cod, and cook over high heat until the cod is barely cooked, about 3 minutes. Return the tofu to the pan, add the scallions, and cook 1 minute more. Season with salt, then slide the tofu and fish onto a platter and garnish with lemon wedges.

2 tablespoons olive oil

1 carton firm tofu, drained and lightly
  pressed (see page 5)

Salt and freshly ground black pepper

3 cooked medium potatoes, diced

1/3 cup diced onion or 4 big scallions,
  including half of the greens, sliced

1 garlic clove, chopped

2 zucchini, diced

1 cup corn kernels, cooked or raw

1 bell pepper, finely diced

2 Roma tomatoes, seeded and diced

2 tablespoons chopped parsley

2 tablespoons chopped basil or
  marjoram

2 whole eggs or 3 egg whites (optional)

1/2 cup grated sharp Cheddar cheese
  (optional)

A scramble, like fried rice or a casserole, can absorb all kinds of vegetables, including any interesting bits and leftovers that might be hiding in the refrigerator. If you wish additional protein, 1 or 2 beaten eggs can be added at the last minute.

1. Heat a nonstick skillet, add 2 teaspoons of the oil, and crumble in the tofu. Cook over medium-high heat, stirring occasionally, until the tofu is dry and lightly browned, 5 to 7 minutes. Season with salt and pepper, turn it into a bowl, and set aside. Return the pan to the heat.

2. Add the remaining oil to the pan and add the next six ingredients. Sauté over high heat until the vegetables are hot and starting to color a bit. Add the tomatoes and herbs. Season the vegetables, then return the tofu to the pan.

3. If using the eggs, pour them over the tofu and vegetables, then cook, while stirring, until they're set. Add the cheese, if using.

Pineapple and Tofu Fried Rice

SERVES 3 TO 4

Whatever happened to fried rice, anyway? It's such a good idea and so easy to make. All kinds of goodies can go into it—a few toasted cashews, small bits of chicken or shrimp, all kinds of vegetables and, of course, tofu. I combine slivers of deep-fried tofu with large pieces of regular tofu that have been sautéed until golden. White rice makes a very pretty background for all the different ingredients, but brown rice is nuttier tasting and better for you. Whichever you choose, start with cold, leftover rice. A mound of steamed napa cabbage or stir-fried tat soi on the side makes a good accompaniment.

2 pieces commercially prepared deep-fried tofu (optional)

1 carton firm tofu, drained

2 tablespoons roasted peanut oil

Salt

1 bunch scallions, including half of the greens, thinly sliced

1 red or yellow bell pepper, diced into small squares

8 snow peas, trimmed and sliced into long strips

3 to 4 cups cooked rice

¼ cup chopped cilantro

5 slices canned pineapple, chopped into large pieces

Soy sauce

2 tablespoons chopped toasted peanuts or roasted cashews

1. Pour 1 cup boiling water over the fried tofu, if using, then slice thinly. Set aside.

2. Blot the fresh tofu with towels to wick up the surface moisture, then cut into cubes of any size you like and blot again. Brush 2 teaspoons peanut oil over a large nonstick skillet, add the tofu, and fry the tofu until golden. Turn it as it cooks so that all the surfaces are nicely colored. Season with salt and remove to a plate. Return the skillet to the heat, add the remaining oil, and turn the heat to high.

3. Add the scallions, bell peppers, and optional deep-fried tofu. Sauté over high heat until the peppers are seared, after a few minutes. Add the snow peas, then crumble in the rice. Continue to sauté until the rice is hot. Add the reserved tofu, half the cilantro and pineapple, and cook several minutes more. Sprinkle over 2 tablespoons soy sauce, or more to taste. Add the chopped nuts, toss once more, then serve with the remaining cilantro scattered over the top.

Fried Rice with Eggs: Beat 2 eggs (or egg whites) with 1 tablespoon soy sauce. When the rice and vegetables are piping hot, pour the eggs over all and stir rapidly so that they coat the rice and are quickly cooked.

1 carton firm or soft tofu

Salt

1 large bunch spinach, stems discarded, leaves well washed

1 jalapeño chile, seeded and coarsely chopped

1 serrano chile, coarsely chopped

1-inch knob ginger, peeled and diced

3 garlic cloves, coarsely chopped

1 cup diced onion

2 tablespoons ghee, butter, or vegetable oil

1 1/2 teaspoons ground cumin

1/8 teaspoon, plus a pinch nutmeg

1/8 teaspoon cayenne pepper

1/2 cup half-and-half

1/3 cup yogurt

Spinach and Tofu Paneer

SERVES 3 TO 4

For a long time it seemed to me that there was more than a superficial resemblance between the white Indian cheese called paneer and tofu. When I finally made the classic Indian dish of spinach and paneer using tofu, it tasted amazingly at home in the cumin, ginger, and chile-laced sauce. There's a little going back and forth between the skillet and a food processor, but this is an easy dish to make. I serve it over rice with a sprinkling of toasted black sesame seeds.

1. Dice the tofu into pieces about the size of a sugar cube or a little smaller. Bring 6 cups water to a boil, add 1 teaspoon salt and lower the heat to a simmer. Add the tofu, turn off the heat, and leave for 4 or 5 minutes. Pour into a colander to drain. (If you've used soft tofu, remove it with a slotted spoon.) Set aside.

2. Steam the spinach until wilted, then remove it to a cutting board and chop. When cool enough to handle, squeeze out the excess water.

3. Put the chiles, ginger, garlic, and onion in a food processor, and process until finely chopped. Heat the ghee or butter in a nonstick skillet, add the onion mixture and cook over medium heat, stirring frequently, for 5 minutes.

4. Add 1 teaspoon salt, the cumin, nutmeg, cayenne, and 1 cup water. Simmer for 5 minutes, then return the mixture to the food processor, add the spinach, and puree.

5. Return the mixture to the skillet, add the half-and-half and the tofu, and simmer for about 5 minutes. Turn off the heat and stir in the yogurt. Serve over basmati rice.

Curries and Braises

....

CURRIES AND BRAISED DISHES provide a gentle cooking atmosphere and time enough in the pan for the tofu to absorb at least a portion of its neighboring herbs and spices. Because the method is not as fast and furious as sautéing or stir-frying, it's not necessary to brown or fry the tofu first. If you enjoy the delicate, nutty flavor of fresh, soft tofu, then braises are a good cooking method. On the other hand, there's nothing that says you can't fry your tofu before adding it to the mix. In some dishes, this can add a definite advantage, particularly a visual one.

Braising also allows flavors of all kinds to join and build a larger harmony. For this very reason, curries provide one of the best ways to utilize tofu, which is right at home with chili pastes, coconut milk, cashews and lime, or Indian tikka spices. You can travel in other directions, too. The Cajun-inspired Cheese, Chile, and Hot Pepper Tofu (page 92) dish works extremely well, as does the mingling of tofu with mushrooms in a paprika-flavored sauce. While none of these big-flavored recipes are very complicated, even simpler examples of gentle cooking are included here, such as simmering tofu in prepared hoisin or oyster sauce. Certainly nothing could be easier!

1 carton firm tofu

2 teaspoons vegetable oil

1/2 white onion, thinly sliced

3 garlic cloves, finely chopped

1 heaping tablespoon ginger, finely chopped

1 jalapeño or serrano chile, seeded and diced

1/2 teaspoon turmeric

1 1/2 teaspoons curry powder

1 cup coconut milk

3 cloves

One 3-inch cinnamon stick

5 green cardamom pods, whole

3 tablespoons chopped cilantro

1/2 teaspoon salt

1 cup fresh or frozen peas

Braised Curried Tofu with Peas

SERVES 3 TO 4

This dish is enormously easy to make. If you heat the tofu in the sauce, then set it aside until you're ready to serve (even as long as overnight, if you wish), the tofu will absorb more of the curry flavors. However, ulti- mately the sauce complements the tofu, and does not disguise it. Serve with busmati rice, yo- gurt, and a spoonful of mango or another favorite chutney.

1. Drain the tofu, then wrap in a towel and press (page 7). Meanwhile, assemble the rest of the ingredients.

2. Heat the oil in a 10-inch casserole or sauté pan. Add the onion and cook over medium heat, stirring occasionally, until the onion is limp and translucent, 3 to 4 minutes. Add the garlic, ginger, chile, turmeric, and curry powder, cook for 2 minutes, then add the coconut milk, spices, cilantro, and salt. Lower the heat and simmer gently while you return to the tofu.

3. Slice the tofu crosswise into slabs about 3/8 inch thick. Slice each slab diagonally into triangles. Give the sauce a stir and taste it for salt. Gently lay the tofu pieces in the pan and spoon the sauce over them. Raise the heat a little and cook until the tofu is heated through, about 5 minutes. Add the peas and cook a few more minutes until they're hot as well.

4. Spoon the tofu and sauce over rice and serve with a spoonful of yo- gurt and chutney.

Fried Tofu and Pepper Curry with Cashews

SERVES 3

Fast and flavorful. Deep-frying the tofu gives the dish a heartier, chewier texture. If you wish to avoid deep-frying, simply shallow-fry the tofu until golden.

1 carton firm tofu

1½ cups peanut oil, for frying

1 small onion, thinly sliced

1 red bell pepper, thinly sliced

2 serrano chiles, minced or finely diced

1 to 2 teaspoons Thai red curry paste

1 cup coconut milk

½ cup Vegetable Stock for Asian Dishes (page 64), chicken stock, or water

Salt

3 tablespoons roasted, chopped cashews

⅓ cup coarsely chopped cilantro leaves

1. Drain the tofu, then wrap in a towel and press (page 7) while you prepare the rest of the ingredients. Cut into 1-inch cubes. If still moist, blot the tofu with toweling so that it won't splatter when fried.

2 Heat the oil in a wok or skillet. When hot enough to sizzle a crumb of tofu, add 6 or 7 pieces and fry until golden and crisp. Don't let them brown, however. You'll need to separate the pieces, as they tend to cling to one another. Remove when done and set on paper towels to drain. Pour all but 1 tablespoon oil out of the wok and return the pan to the heat.

3. Add the onion, bell pepper, and chiles, and stir-fry for 1 minute. Stir in the curry paste, then add the coconut milk, stock, ½ teaspoon salt, and the tofu. Simmer 2 minutes more, or until the tofu is heated through. Serve over rice or noodles, garnished with the roasted cashews and cilantro.

1 carton soft or firm tofu

1 can coconut milk mixed with ¹/₂ cup
    water, chicken broth, or stock

2 teaspoons light brown sugar

¹/₂ teaspoon salt

1 tablespoon ground coriander

2 teaspoons curry powder

¹/₂ teaspoon turmeric

¹/₄ teaspoon cayenne pepper

1 teaspoon tamarind paste dissolved
    in ¹/₂ cup hot water

2 large garlic cloves, crushed or
    finely chopped

1 heaping tablespoon finely
    chopped ginger

4 Roma tomatoes, seeded and diced

4 scallions, including the firm greens,
    chopped

Juice of 1 lime

Mushroom soy sauce, to taste

Chopped cilantro

Coconut Curry with Tofu and Lime

SERVES 3 TO 4

I like the clean taste of the un-fried tofu when it meets the sharp, sour flavors of lime juice and tamarind. Serve over rice with a shower of chopped cilantro.

1. Drain the tofu, then dice it into ¹/₂-inch cubes.

2. Combine the next ten ingredients in a 10 inch skillet. Bring to a boil and simmer for 1 minute. Add the tofu, lower the heat, and simmer, covered, for 10 minutes. Add the tomatoes and scallions, and simmer 5 minutes more.

3. Add the lime juice. Season to taste with a teaspoon or more mushroom soy sauce. Serve garnished with chopped cilantro.

Silken Tofu in Spicy Red Coconut Sauce

SERVES 4

This couldn't be quicker to assemble, so be sure to have your rice cooked or your pasta water boiling before you begin. For a completely different visual effect, cut the tofu into large cubes or triangles instead of into tiny cubes.

1 cup dry basmati rice or 8 ounces Chinese egg noodles

2 boxes firm silken tofu or 1 carton soft tofu

2 teaspoons roasted peanut oil

2 large garlic cloves, minced

1 tablespoon finely chopped ginger

1 bunch scallions, including some of the firm greens, sliced into rounds

1 can coconut milk

2 tablespoons mushroom soy or regular soy sauce

1 to 2 teaspoons Thai red curry paste, or more to taste

4 large basil leaves, slivered

1. First, begin cooking the rice or put up the water for the pasta. Dice the tofu into small cubes, about 1/3 inch across.

2. Heat the oil in a wide, nonstick skillet. Add the garlic, ginger, and scallions, and stir-fry for 1 minute.

3. Add the coconut milk and soy sauce, then stir in the curry paste, adding more to taste if you like it really hot. Add the tofu and simmer until heated through.

4. Spoon over the cooked rice or noodles and garnish with the basil leaves.

One can coconut milk,
    light or regular
1 to 2 teaspoons Thai red chili paste,
    to taste
1½ tablespoons brown sugar
2 tablespoons soy sauce, preferably
    mushroom soy
1½ teaspoons curry powder
1 carton or 2 boxes firm tofu, diced into
    large cubes
1 bunch scallions, including some of
    the greens, sliced into large pieces
    on the diagonal

4 large shiitake mushrooms, thickly
    sliced on an angle
4 Roma tomatoes, cut into sixths
1 golden or orange bell pepper,
    thinly sliced
¼ cup basil leaves, torn into
    dime-sized pieces
Salt
1 bunch spinach, leaves only, coarsely
    chopped and well washed
1½ cups white or brown basmati
    rice (pages 120–121)

Braised Late Summer Vegetables and Tofu

SERVES 4

Late summer is an especially good time to make this stew—there's still fresh basil (look for the Thai basil or opal basil), good tomatoes, and the last of the bell peppers. Yet cool weather makes this mélange especially appealing. You can use the aseptically packed silken tofu here or regular soft or firm tofu. Serve over rice.

1. Empty the coconut milk into a wide saucepan, then fill the can halfway with water, swish it around, and add it to the pan. Set over medium heat and whisk in half the chili paste, sugar, soy sauce, and curry powder. Taste and add more chili paste if you want it hotter. Bring to a boil, then lower the heat and simmer for 5 minutes.

2. Add the tofu, vegetables, basil, and a pinch or two of salt. Stew gently for 5 minutes, then add the spinach and cook until wilted and bright green. Serve over the rice. ●

Cauliflower and Tofu with Tikka Spices

SERVES 4

The Indian spices used for grilled tandoori lamb or chicken turn tofu an inviting red-orange hue. Because the spices don't penetrate into the tofu, I cut it into pieces about ³/₄ inch long and about half that wide so there's plenty of surface area to coat.

1 carton firm tofu

1¹/₂ cups white or brown basmati rice (pages 120–121)

1 small cauliflower, cut into small florets

•

Spice Mix

2 teaspoons garam masala

2 teaspoons ground cumin

1 teaspoon ground coriander

¹/₂ teaspoon turmeric

¹/₂ teaspoon nutmeg

¹/₄ teaspoon ground cardamom

¹/₈ teaspoon ground cloves

1 teaspoon ground red chile or hot paprika

•

2 tablespoons vegetable oil

Salt

¹/₄ cup finely chopped or ground cashews

1 can coconut milk, light or regular

1 garlic clove, pressed or minced

¹/₄ cup chopped cilantro

¹/₂ cup drained yogurt

2 scallions, thinly sliced

Mango or other chutney

1. Drain and press the tofu (page 7), then begin cooking the rice. Steam the cauliflower until tender, but not cooked all the way through. Rinse and set aside. Assemble the ingredients for the spice mix and place them in a pie plate.

2. Slice the tofu into rectangles about ³/₄ inch long and about half as wide. If the tofu is still damp, blot it further with a paper towel, then coat it with the spice mix.

3. Heat the oil in a wide skillet. Add the tofu, season with ½ teaspoon salt, and cook over medium-high heat for 4 minutes. The surface will be browning, but it's hard to see through the color of the spices. Turn the tofu a few times so that it browns evenly.

4. Add the cashews, coconut milk, and garlic to the pan. Slide the pan back and forth to pick up all the spices and distribute everything evenly, then reduce the heat so that the milk just simmers. Add the cauliflower and cook, covered, until it's warmed through and tender, about 5 minutes. Taste for salt and stir in the cilantro.

5. Divide the rice among 4 plates and spoon the curry and its sauce on top. Spoon some yogurt over each serving and sprinkle scallions over all. Add a spoonful of chutney on the side or pass it separately.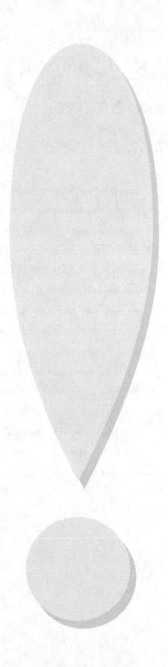

Tofu with Cumin Laced Spinach and Shrimp

SERVES 4

Based on an Indian recipe but made with tofu, this recipe translates even better if you include a few shrimp on each serving. I use soft tofu that is simmered in salted water, then drained and sprinkled with turmeric. It's the most flavorful tofu, but being so tender, it's a little tricky to handle. If you prefer, use firm tofu—either regular or silken—instead. Sauté the shrimp separately at the last minute and serve them as a garnish.

1½ to 2 cartons soft tofu

Salt

1½ teaspoons turmeric

2 tablespoons, plus 2 teaspoons vegetable oil

5 large garlic cloves, chopped (about 2 tablespoons)

1½ teaspoons roasted, ground cumin

1 large jalapeño chile, finely diced

2 heaping tablespoons chopped ginger

2 large onions, finely diced

12 large shrimp, shelled and deveined

Juice of 1 lime

½ cup fresh or frozen peas

1 large bunch spinach, leaves washed and chopped but not dried

2 tablespoons chopped cilantro

3 cups cooked white rice

1. Cut the tofu into 1 inch cubes. Bring 4 to 6 cups water to a boil and add 1 teaspoon salt. Reduce the heat so that the water is barely simmering, then lower the tofu into the pan. Cook for 4 minutes, then remove with a strainer and set on a towel to drain while you prepare the vegetables. Once the tofu is dry, sprinkle with ½ teaspoon turmeric.

2. Heat 2 tablespoons of the oil in a wide skillet set over medium-high heat. Add the garlic and cumin and cook, stirring, until the garlic is pale gold. Add the chile, ginger, onions, another ½ teaspoon turmeric and continue cooking until the onions are lightly colored and soft, 5 to 7 minutes. If the pan seems too dry at any point, add water in ½ cup increments and reduce the heat. While the onion is cooking, rinse the shrimp, then pat them dry. Toss them with the remaining turmeric and half the lime juice. Set aside until you're ready to serve.

3. Add the peas and the spinach to the onions. Turn the heat to high, sprinkle with 1/2 teaspoon salt, and cook until wilted. Nestle the tofu into the vegetables, add a half cup water, then cover and cook until the tofu is heated through, about 4 minutes.

4. Heat the remaining oil in a wide skillet. When hot, add the shrimp, sprinkle with salt, and sauté over high heat, turning a few times, until they're red and firm when pressed with a finger.

5. Serve the vegetables over cooked rice with 3 shrimp arranged on each serving. Sprinkle over the remaining lime juice, garnish with the cilantro, and serve.

Tofu Simmered
in Hoisin Sauce

SERVES 2 TO 4

Because hoisin sauce is usually rather sweet, dice the tofu very small and serve it as a sauce with rice, with stir-fried spinach, green beans, or broccoli on the side. For a more eye-catching appearance, cut the tofu into triangles, brown them briefly in a little oil, then simmer in the sauce.

1 carton firm or soft tofu (See Note)

5 teaspoons roasted peanut oil

1/3 cup hoisin sauce

1 tablespoon thin or light soy sauce

1 tablespoon rice wine or sherry

1 garlic clove, minced

1/2 teaspoon freshly ground black pepper

1/2 cup water, chicken stock, or vegetable stock

1 tablespoon black or white sesame seeds, toasted in a small skillet

1 scallion, including the 3 inches of the greens, thinly sliced diagonally

1. Drain the firm tofu, wrap it in a towel and press while you assemble the ingredients for the sauce. Slice it crosswise a scant 1/2 inch thick, then into triangles. Blot with paper toweling.

2. Heat a nonstick skillet, brush with 2 teaspoons of the oil, then add the tofu. Fry over medium-high heat until golden, then turn, adding another 2 teaspoons oil, and brown the second side.

3. Combine the hoisin sauce, soy sauce, rice wine, garlic, pepper, and remaining 1 teaspoon oil. Stir in the water or stock, then pour the mixture over the tofu and shuffle the pan back and forth to distribute it evenly. Cook over medium heat until bubbling and slightly reduced, about 2 minutes. Garnish with the sesame seeds and scallion.

Note: Soft tofu packed in water has the nicest flavor and texture, both of which are more pronounced if the tofu isn't browned. If you enjoy the pure flavor of the soft tofu, heat the sauce with the tofu in it until it has warmed through. If it reduces too much, simply add a little more water or stock to thin it out.

1 carton soft or firm tofu, drained

2 cups vegetable stock, chicken stock, or water

3 tablespoons oyster sauce

5 teaspoons rice wine or sherry

2 teaspoons soy sauce

1 teaspoon sugar

2 teaspoons cornstarch

1 tablespoon peanut oil

2 teaspoons minced ginger

Soft Tofu with Oyster Sauce

SERVES 3 TO 4

1. Cut the tofu into 1-inch cubes or, if you prefer, smaller ones the size of sugar lumps.

2. Combine the next five ingredients in a bowl. Mix the cornstarch with 1 tablespoon water.

3. Heat a wok or large skillet. Add the oil and when it's hot, add the ginger and the sauce ingredients. Bring to a boil, stir to dissolve the sugar, and simmer for about 1 minute. Add the tofu, cover, and simmer until heated through, 3 to 5 minutes, depending on the size of the cubes. Slide the pan back and forth to coat it with the sauce. Stir the diluted cornstarch into the pan and cook until it thickens, in just 1 or 2 minutes.

This dish is for those who appreciate the flavor and texture of soft tofu. If you use firm tofu, brown it according to the previous recipe, then proceed. Serve with rice or noodles and stir-fried greens such as choy sum, bok choy, or spinach. In summer, grilled Japanese eggplants, halved and placed around the rice and tofu, would be a good choice.

Hot Pot with Bean Threads, Soft Tofu, and Chinese Greens

SERVES 2

This is a main-course mélange of vegetables, glassy noodles, and soft tofu simmered in broth. Additional seasoning, one that's on the spicy side, comes from Lan Chi Chilli Paste with Soybeans. You could also stir in a little oyster sauce or hoisin sauce if you want more zip to this delicate mushroom-laced broth, but it's quite nice as it is. Use a wide pan with curved or sloping sides, a casserole, or very wide skillet to make this dish.

6 dried shiitake mushrooms

2 ounces mung bean threads or thin rice sticks

1 pound bok choy, napa cabbage, or spinach leaves, cut into 1 inch ribbons

2 carrots, peeled and sliced diagonally or roll-cut

1 bunch scallions, including the firm greens, cut into 1 inch pieces

1 carton soft or firm tofu, drained

2 teaspoons sugar

1/2 teaspoon salt

2 tablespoons soy sauce

1 1/2 cups chicken stock or vegetable stock

3 tablespoons rice wine or sherry

1 tablespoon roasted peanut oil

1 heaping tablespoon minced ginger

1 heaping tablespoon minced garlic

2 to 4 teaspoons Lan Chi Chilli Paste with Soybeans or oyster sauce (optional)

1. Cover the dried mushrooms with ¾ cup boiling water and set aside. Cover the mung bean threads or rice sticks with warm water and set aside to soften.

2. Prepare the vegetables and group them on a platter. Drain the tofu and cut it into 1-inch cubes. Remove the mushrooms from the water and squeeze, reserving the soaking water, and strain. Remove the stems and slice the caps into strips. Combine the sugar, salt, soy sauce, rice wine, mushroom water, and stock in a bowl.

3. Heat a wide pan and add the oil. Swirl it around and when hot, add the ginger and garlic and stir-fry for 30 seconds. Add the vegetables, broth, and the mung bean threads, minus their soaking water. Nestle the tofu into the bean threads, and gently bring to a boil. Reduce the heat and simmer, covered, for 15 minutes.

4. Remove and taste the broth, adding more soy sauce or salt, if desired. Stir in the chilli paste, if using, dabbing it into different parts of the pan so that it will season the broth evenly. Taste and add more if you wish. Serve in 2 large bowls.

1 carton firm tofu, drained

2 tablespoons peanut or sesame oil, for frying

Creamy Nut Butter Sauce

2 scallions including the greens, thinly sliced on the diagonal

1 tablespoon toasted white or black sesame seeds

SERVES 2 TO 4

1. Slice the tofu crosswise into scant $1/2$-inch slabs, then cut each slab into 2 triangles. Blot with paper towels.

2. Heat a large cast-iron or nonstick skillet and add the oil. When hot, add the tofu and fry over medium-high heat until golden. Turn and cook on the second side.

3. Meanwhile, combine the ingredients for the sauce. When the tofu is done, pour in half the sauce and cook until bubbling and partially reduced. Turn off the heat, scatter the scallions and sesame seeds over the top, and bring to the table.

Here triangles of tofu are pan-fried, simmered briefly in half the nut butter sauce, and garnished with slivered scallion and sesame seeds. The rest of the sauce can be spooned over brown rice, noodles, or whatever you choose as an accompaniment. If possible, present the tofu in the pan that it's cooked in.

The Creamy Nut Butter Sauce

$1/4$ cup regular soy sauce

1 tablespoon tamari

$1/4$ cup sesame paste, peanut butter, or cashew butter

2 tablespoons rice wine vinegar

2 tablespoons white or light brown sugar

$1/2$ teaspoon red pepper flakes or chili oil

2 scallions, finely chopped

$1/3$ cup water or stock

Pinch salt

Combine all the ingredients in a small food processor and puree until smooth. Taste for salt and add a little extra, if needed.

Tofu and Mushrooms Braised in a Sweet-and-Sour Sauce

SERVES 4

To give the tofu some color and visual distinction, I brown it in a nonstick or cast-iron pan just barely coated with oil, or, for more chewiness, deep-fry it until golden. The inclusion of snow peas, broccoli florets, yellow squash, braised spinach, or another brightly colored and simply cooked vegetable added at the end make the dish much more vibrant.

The Sauce

2 heaping tablespoons Dijon mustard

2 tablespoons Worcestershire sauce

2 tablespoons molasses or brown sugar

1 tablespoon mushroom soy, tamari, or regular soy sauce

1 tablespoon tomato paste

3/4 cup red wine

2 large garlic cloves, pressed

1/3 cup water

The Tofu and Vegetables

One carton regular or firm tofu, drained

5 teaspoons peanut oil

Salt and freshly ground black pepper

1 large onion, diced into 1/2-inch squares

1 red bell pepper, cut into large, irregular pieces

1 yellow bell pepper, cut into large, irregular pieces

1/4 teaspoon dried thyme

12 ounces mushrooms (mixed brown, white, and shiitake are good)

2 Roma tomatoes, peeled and diced

2 cups snow peas, broccoli florets, or other vegetable

1/4 cup chopped parsley or cilantro

1. Combine all the sauce ingredients in a bowl and set aside.

2. Cut the tofu into 1-inch cubes. Heat a nonstick skillet and brush with 1 teaspoon of the oil. Add the tofu and cook over medium-high heat until golden-brown on the bottom. Turn and cook until the other surfaces are golden as well. Season with salt and pepper and set aside.

3. Add the remaining oil to a wide pot, such as a Dutch oven. Turn the heat to high, add the onion, bell peppers, and thyme. Cook, stirring occasionally, until they begin to brown in places and a film appears on the bottom of the pot, after several minutes. Be sure to let the ingredients cook *without* stirring for ½-minute intervals so that they'll brown. You can use this time to quarter the mushrooms and prepare the snow peas or broccoli.

4. Add the mushrooms and continue cooking, again stirring occasionally, until they are seared in places. Add 1 teaspoon salt and grind in plenty of black pepper. Once a number of the mushrooms have gained some color, stir in the sauce, scraping up the goodies from the bottom of the pan. Reduce the heat to low, lay the tofu over the vegetables, and cover the pot. Cook for 15 minutes. During the last 5 minutes add the tomatoes.

5. Blanch the snow peas or broccoli florets in boiling salted water.

6. Stir in the parsley and spoon the vegetables and their sauce over rice or noodles, adding the snow peas last.

Cheese, Chile, and Hot Pepper Tofu

SERVES 4 TO 6

I've borrowed widely here in an attempt to introduce some Louisiana flavors to tofu. This is not a lean dish, but it's far more so than the recipe I started working from! Serve this over plain white rice. The recipe may look formidable, but it's not at all difficult to put together.

1 carton firm tofu, drained

The Seasoning Mix

2 teaspoons salt, plus extra to taste

1 teaspoon dry mustard

1/2 teaspoon cayenne pepper

1 teaspoon paprika

1/2 teaspoon freshly ground white pepper

1 teaspoon freshly ground black pepper

1/2 teaspoon ground cumin

1/2 teaspoon dried thyme

1/2 teaspoon dried oregano

1/4 teaspoon cinnamon

2 tablespoons flour

The Vegetables

3 tablespoons vegetable oil, or more if needed

2 onions, diced into 1/2-inch squares

2 green bell peppers, cut into 1/2-inch pieces

1 yellow bell pepper, cut into 1/2-inch pieces

2 long green chiles, such as Anaheims, roasted, seeded, and chopped

1 bay leaf

2 large garlic cloves, finely chopped

2 1/2 cups vegetable or chicken stock

1/2 cup sour cream

1 cup grated Muenster or Jack cheese

Chopped parsley

4 to 6 cups cooked rice

1. Press the tofu while you assemble the seasonings and prepare the vegetables. Then slice the tofu in half, parallel to the cutting board, but don't separate the pieces. Cutting from the top, slice the tofu into 5 or 6 triangles. You'll have a total of 10 or 12 pieces. Separate them and blot with a paper towel if they look damp in the center. Set aside 1 teaspoon of the seasoning mix and put the rest in a pie pan. Dip the tofu into the seasoning, coating it generously.

2. Heat 2 tablespoons of the oil in a cast-iron or other heavy skillet. When hot, add the tofu in a single layer. (You may have to do this in two batches, using extra oil.) Fry over medium heat without disturbing for several minutes until crusty and well browned, then turn and brown on the other side. (You can even brown them on the edges standing the pieces upright against the sides of the pan.) Remove to a plate when finished.

3. Return the skillet to the heat without washing it—you want those crusty bits remaining on the bottom of the pan—and add another tablespoon of oil. When hot, add the onions, bell peppers, roasted chiles, bay leaf, garlic, and reserved seasoning mix. Cook over high heat, stirring frequently, until the onions start to brown, 8 to 10 minutes. If the pan should become dry and sticky before the onions are done, add $1/2$ cup of the stock and scrape vigorously to pick up the bits on the bottom. They will immediately thicken the liquid and lend their color. Taste for salt.

4. Lay the tofu on top of the vegetables. Add enough stock just to come up to the tofu without covering it. Bring to a boil, reduce the heat to low, and cover the pan. Simmer for 15 minutes.

5. Set several of the nicer-looking pieces of tofu aside and turn off the heat. Spoon several tablespoons of the liquid into the sour cream and stir until smooth, then stir the mixture into the pan. Next, stir in the cheese and let it melt. Return the pieces of tofu to the stew, add some fresh chopped parsley, and serve, in its pan, with rice.

PASTA (AND NOODLES), the universal food, is at home with tofu as it is with other foods, whether you're pairing tofu with spaghetti, mung bean threads or buckwheat pasta, or whether you're using ginger, chile, and soy, or sour cream and dill as seasonings and sauces.

Chilled *soba* and tofu have already met in the salad chapter, where they mingle with soy, ginger, and dark-roasted sesame oil. In a more discrete fashion, many of the tofu-based sauces can be used to coat a macaroni salad or salads based on somen or *udon* noodles. However, most of my pasta-tofu combinations are warm dishes and none of them feature tofu as a replacement for mozzarella or ricotta cheese. Instead, I've tried to feature tofu as itself, although recipes involving chicken and fish have proved more than once to be worthwhile as springboards.

There's no one best way of using tofu with pasta or noodles. It needn't be fried first, although sometimes it works best that way. It needn't always be cut into large pieces. The Seared Mushrooms with Tiny Cubes of Tofu (page 97) makes the most delicious filling for *wonton* wrappers, an intriguing mixture that can also be tossed with thin Chinese egg noodles. Thicker Chinese egg noodles are feature with glazed tofu and a peanut sauce. Curly American egg noodles make a tender bed for a sauce of tofu, sour cream, and paprika, while lo mein noodles drink up the tamarind-laced sauce that accompanies sautéed Mushrooms and Tofu on page 100. Although I haven't called for them, I think saffron noodles would make a rather interesting base for any of the tofu curries, especially those involving coconut milk. No doubt there's a type of pasta or noodle for virtually every tofu dish, even those where rice has been suggested as an accompaniment.

1/2 cup sour cream

1 carton firm tofu, drained

Salt and freshly ground black pepper

1 tablespoon vegetable oil

1 tablespoon butter

1 onion, finely diced

1 pound mushrooms, sliced about

   1/3 inch thick

Juice of 1/2 lemon

1 tablespoon flour

11/2 tablespoons mild (sweet) paprika

1/3 cup white wine or sherry

2/3 cup water, vegetable, or

   chicken stock

2 tablespoons chopped dill or

   1 tablespoon chopped tarragon

8 ounces egg noodles

Mushrooms and Tofu in Paprika Cream over Egg Noodles

SERVES 4

I wasn't sure how successfully tofu could replace chicken in this dish, but it turns out that paprika, sour cream, and dill are good seasonings for both. Not only is this an especially satisfying dish to eat, it's easy to make, even on a busy week night.

1. Let the sour cream come to room temperature.

2. Dice the tofu into 1/2-inch cubes. Set a nonstick or cast-iron skillet over medium-high heat and brush lightly with oil. Add the tofu and cook until golden on the bottom, about 3 minutes. Turn to brown the other sides. Sprinkle with salt and pepper, then remove to a dish.

3. Add the oil and butter to the pan. When it foams, add the onion and mushrooms, squeezing the lemon over the mushrooms so that they keep their color. Cook until the mushrooms are browned and the onions are soft, about 8 minutes. Add the tofu and gently mix together.

4. Sprinkle over the flour and paprika, then season with 1/2 teaspoon salt and pepper. Turn the mixture to incorporate the flour, and add the wine, let it bubble up, then reduce until syrupy. Add the water, reduce the heat to medium-low, and cook, covered, for 15 minutes. Check once or twice to make sure there's enough liquid to make a little sauce. If not, add more water or stock as needed. Taste for salt. Cook the egg noodles until al dente, then drain and place on a warmed platter.

5. Rewarm the sauce, if necessary, then turn off the heat, add the fresh herb and stir in the sour cream. Pour over the egg noodles and serve.

Mushroom Tortellini with Light Tarragon Cream Sauce

MAKES 32 TORTELLINI

"You mean that's tofu in there?" asked one of my guests when biting into these succulent little pastas. The filling, given as a separate recipe below, is so delicious I'm lucky if it ever makes it into the wrappers. There's no reason you couldn't toss the filling with strands of wholewheat pasta or thin Chinese egg noodles along with the cream sauce or a rich mushroom broth. Another variant is to use steamed napa cabbage leaves as a wrap instead, making pale green bundles of succulent mushrooms and tofu.

The Filling

Seared Mushrooms with Tiny Cubes
   of Tofu (page 97)

•

32 wonton wrappers
2 cups half-and-half or a mixture of
   half-and-half and cream
2 shallots, finely diced
1 tablespoon chopped fresh tarragon
2 teaspoons mushroom soy sauce,
   to taste
Salt and freshly ground black pepper
2 cups napa cabbage, sliced into
   narrow ribbons

1. Prepare the filling and spread it on a plate and refrigerate until completely cool.

2. Place a wonton wrapper on the counter, put 1 teaspoon of the filling in the center, brush the edges with water, then fold, corner to corner, to make a triangle. Press the edges to make sure they're sealed. Take the two ends of the triangle and fold them so that one end rests on the other end. Seal with another drop of water. Set them on a sheet pan dusted with rice flour or on nonstick pastry paper.

3. Simmer the half-and-half in a wide skillet with the remaining ingredients for 5 minutes. Season with a few pinches of salt and black pepper. Meanwhile, simmer the tortellini in salted, simmering water for 2 minutes, or until tender, then remove with a strainer and set them in the sauce. Shuffle the pan back and forth so that the sauce washes over the pasta. Continue to cook a little longer if the sauce is still on the thin side. Place on heated plates, pour the sauce and cabbage over each plate, then serve, adding a little ground pepper to each plate.

1 carton soft or firm tofu, drained and
    diced into $1/4$-inch cubes
2 tablespoons brown sugar
2 tablespoons water
4 teaspoons mushroom soy sauce
$1/2$ teaspoon sea salt
3 tablespoons coarsely chopped garlic

3 tablespoons chopped tarragon
1 teaspoon freshly ground black pepper
3 tablespoons, plus 2 teaspoons olive oil
1 pound brown Italian mushrooms,
    chopped in small pieces
4 large shallots or 1 small onion,
    finely diced

Seared Mushrooms with Tiny Cubes of Tofu

MAKES 2 CUPS

1. Simmer the tofu for 2 minutes in salted water, then set on paper toweling to dry while you prepare the rest of the ingredients. Combine the sugar, water, mushroom soy sauce, and salt in a cup and set aside. Chop the garlic, tarragon, and pepper to make a coarse paste or mixture.

2. Heat 3 tablespoons oil in a 10 inch skillet. When hot, add the garlic-tarragon-pepper mixture and cook for about 30 seconds. Immediately add the mushrooms, give them a stir, then sauté until they're well browned and their juices have been released then reabsorbed, about 7 minutes. Scrape them into a bowl.

3. Heat the remaining oil in the skillet and add the tofu. Cook over medium-high heat, shaking the pan every few minutes, until the cubes are golden. Return the mushrooms to the pan and add the shallots.

4. Add the reserved liquid to the pan and stir rapidly, cooking until everything is well mixed and still moist. Remove from the heat. Taste for salt and pepper.

Chinese Noodles with Glazed Tofu and Peanut Sauce

SERVES 2 TO 4

While I try to avoid recipes that send you scooting to other parts of the book, both the tofu and the peanut sauce are so easy to make that this isn't terribly complicated or time-consuming. This rather rich and filling dish is best served in smallish portions. Fresh Chinese noodles in plastic packages can often be found in the vegetable section of grocery stores. The thick or wide-cut noodles are good choices for this sturdy dish.

8 to 10 ounces fresh Chinese noodles, thick or wide-cut

Glazed Tofu (page 17), cut into strips about 1/2 inch wide and 1/4 inch thick

1/2 recipe Peanut Sauce (page 32) or a commercial peanut sauce

4 scallions, including a few inches of the greens, sliced on the diagonal

3 tablespoons chopped cilantro

1. Bring 4 quarts water to a boil for the pasta. Open the package and fluff the strands of noodles with your fingers. While the water is heating, prepare the tofu, the peanut sauce, and the garnishes.

2. Add the noodles to the water, give it a stir, and cook until tender but not mushy. Check the package instructions. Reserve 2 cups of the cooking water, then drain the noodles and rinse with *hot* water.

3. Immediately put the pasta in a wide skillet along with the tofu. Thin the sauce with the reserved water, pour it over the noodles, and toss repeatedly with two forks. Add most of the scallions and cilantro and toss again. Divide among heated bowls and garnish with the remaining scallions and cilantro.

1 package soba noodles (about
    8 ounces)
1 bunch slender scallions, including
    a few inches of the greens
1½ tablespoons white or black
    sesame seeds
1 carton fresh silken or soft tofu or
    2 boxes firm-silken tofu

The Sauce

6 tablespoons soy sauce, such as
    Kikkoman or thin Chinese soy sauce
2 tablespoons rice wine vinegar
1½ teaspoons dark sesame oil
1 teaspoon sugar, or more to taste
1 tablespoon finely minced ginger

Chilled Soba with Soft Tofu and Soy–Sesame Sauce

MAKES 4 APPETIZERS OR 2 TO 3 MAIN-DISH SERVINGS

1. Cook the noodles in boiling water until tender but still retain a texture, about 6 to 8 minutes. Drain and rinse under cold water to stop the cooking and cool. Shake off the excess water. (If you're cooking the noodles ahead of time, refrigerate them.) Trim the scallions and slice them very thinly. Toast the sesame seeds in a dry skillet over medium heat until fragrant, then transfer to a dish and set aside. Carefully open the tofu and turn it onto a cutting board to drain while you make the sauce.

2. Combine the ingredients for the sauce in a bowl. Taste to make sure the balance of oil to vinegar is the way you like it. It may seem salty, but remember that it's going on tofu.

3. Toss the noodles with half the scallions and sesame seeds, then divide among 4 plates. Make a little depression in the center of the noodles. Dice the tofu into ½-inch cubes and set them in the center. Spoon the sauce over the tofu and the noodles, then sprinkle with the remaining scallions and sesame seeds. Serve.

An ideal dish for a hot day, these noodles and tofu are cool, light and refreshing and couldn't be easier to make.

The sauce can be used as a dipping sauce for tofu (cooked or raw) without the noodles. Plus you can vary it by adding a tablespoon of peanut butter or tahini. Or, for a sauce that's a little more substantial, add ½ teaspoon chili oil to make it a little spicy.

I especially like the silken tofu that is not aseptically packaged, such as that made by Azumaya.

Sautéed Mushrooms and Tofu with Tamarind Sauce

SERVES 3 TO 4

Tamarind gives this sauce a pleasing sourish edge. Equally good over lo mein noodles or fettuccine; be sure to start the pasta water first, so that the pasta will be cooked about the time the dish is done. If the finished dish sits, the mushrooms and tofu will soak up the juices. It's much better if they can mix with the noodles.

1 carton firm tofu, drained

1 tablespoon tamarind paste diluted in 1 cup warm water

Salt and freshly ground black pepper

1 teaspoon sugar

2 tablespoons peanut or canola oil

8 ounces shiitake mushrooms or brown Italian mushrooms, stems removed, caps halved or quartered if large

1 small white onion, diced

2 teaspoons minced garlic

1 tablespoon mushroom soy or tamari

1 jalapeño chile, seeded and finely diced

2 Roma tomatoes, seeded and neatly diced

8 ounces lo mein noodles or fettuccine

Chopped parsley

1. Cut the tofu crosswise into slices 1-inch wide and set on cloth or paper toweling while you assemble the rest of the ingredients. Bring water for the pasta to a boil. Returning to the tofu, blot it once more, then cut into 1-inch cubes. Sprinkle them with salt, plenty of pepper, and the sugar. Dilute the tamarind paste in the water by first mashing it into just a few tablespoons water, then gradually adding the remainder. Start cooking the pasta.

2. Heat a wide skillet over a high flame. Add half the oil, and when it's hot, add the tofu. Let it rest in the pan for at least a minute, then carefully turn. Brown all the sides. In all this will take 8 to 10 minutes. With the sugar, it should turn a rich golden brown. When done, remove it to a plate.

3. Return the pan to the heat, add the remaining oil, then when hot, add the mushrooms, onion, and garlic. Cook over high heat, stirring frequently, until the mushrooms are seared and fragrant, 3 to 4 minutes. Return the tofu to the pan, add the tamarind and soy sauce, and boil until reduced by about half. The dish will look quite dark, and there should be plenty of liquid in the pan. Season with 1/2 teaspoon salt and plenty of freshly ground pepper. Add the chile and tomato, give a quick stir, and turn off the heat.

4. Drain the pasta and divide among 3 or 4 heated bowls. Spoon the tofu and mushrooms on top and serve with a little chopped parsley on each.

Stir-fried Noodles with Fresh and Baked Tofu

SERVES 4 TO 6

You'll need a big wok or two skillets to hold this large stir-fry. Here's a recipe where you can put that very dense, baked tofu to good use. Choose tofu that's been flavored with star anise or five-spice powder, available in natural food stores. It has an entirely different texture than fresh—it's quite meaty, actually. I find it tastes best if you slice it thinly and stir-fry it with the ginger and garlic.

The Sauce

2 tablespoons soy sauce
2 tablespoons tamari
3 tablespoons hoisin or oyster sauce
¼ cup stock or water
1 tablespoon rice wine or sherry
2 teaspoons sugar
¼ cup coarsely chopped cilantro, plus long, pretty sprigs for garnish

One 8- to 10-ounce package Chinese wide-cut egg noodles
1 carton firm tofu, drained and cut into large cubes
2½ tablespoons roasted peanut oil
1 heaping tablespoon chopped ginger
1 heaping tablespoon chopped garlic
1 jalapeño chile, seeded and diced
2 chunks baked tofu, thinly sliced
1 onion, thinly sliced
6 shiitake mushrooms, stems discarded, thinly sliced
1 large broccoli, the head cut into florets, the stem peeled and sliced
1 red or yellow bell pepper, cut into narrow strips, then halved
2 carrots, peeled and thinly sliced
Salt
4 ounces snow peas, trimmed
1 bunch scallions, including the firm greens, cut into 1-inch lengths

1. Mix the sauce ingredients together and set aside.

2. Bring a pot of water to boil for the noodles and tofu. Reduce it to a simmer, add the cubed tofu and simmer gently for 4 minutes. Lift out the tofu with a strainer and set aside. Return the water to a boil, add the noodles and cook until tender-firm, following the package directions. Drain and rinse under cold water. Toss with 1 tablespoon of the oil and set aside.

3. Set a wok or skillet over high heat. Add the remaining oil, swirl it around. When hot, add the ginger, garlic, chile, and baked tofu. Stir-fry for 1 minute, then add onion, mushrooms, broccoli, bell pepper, and carrots. Season with a few pinches of salt and stir-fry, rapidly tossing the vegetables in their pan, for 3 minutes.

4. Now add the snow peas, scallions, and boiled tofu. Stir-fry for 1 minute more, then add the noodles and the sauce. Reduce the heat, toss so that everything is evenly mingled, then cover and cook until the noodles are heated through, a matter of just a few minutes. Turn onto a large platter and garnish with sprigs of cilantro.

ONCE WHEN I WAS LOOKING FOR LUNCH in Baja, Mexico, I noticed a sign advertising "soy chorizo." I found it surprising, but since then I've also found soy chorizo advertised elsewhere in Mexico. I discovered in a Mexican health food store, that it was made of TVP, or texturized vegetable protein, seasoned with chorizo spices. The sausage I tried in the market was absolutely delicious. Most likely, the TVP was used as an extender and mixed with pork. Nonetheless, it inspired me to make an attempt at using tofu in sausage and, the result is a delicious crumble that's right at home with scrambled eggs or in a breakfast burrito. If you want a "sausage" that will stick together, add some moistened bread crumbs and eggs. I've included both methods here. While I've stayed with Mexican seasonings, if you like the idea, try using the seasonings that go into your favorite sausages—cumin, fennel seed, chile—whatever you prefer.

Tofu also works well as scrambled eggs. If you use a soft tofu and just break it into the pan, you'll end up with tender curds; firmer tofu will give you denser ones. Just a pinch or two of turmeric or curry softens the glaring white color of the tofu, giving it a light golden hue. This is one instance where additions such as cheese, scallions, herbs, and salsas fit right in. You can also break an egg or two, or just the whites, into the pan once the tofu is cooked. I ate scrambled tofu with egg whites for a week at the Rancho la Puerta fitness spa and never realized I was eating tofu (and me, a tofu fan!), so that just goes to show you how well it can work.

1 carton extra-firm or firm tofu

2 teaspoons chipotle chile powder, ground red chile, or hot paprika

1 tablespoon mushroom soy sauce

1/2 cup red wine vinegar

6 medium garlic cloves

1 teaspoon fresh oregano, roasted

1 teaspoon ground cumin seeds

1/2 teaspoon coriander seeds

1 poblano chile, roasted

2 cups chard leaves or beet greens

1 cup chopped cilantro

1 cup chopped parsley

1 cup bread crumbs

1 teaspoon salt

2 eggs (optional)

1. Crumble the tofu so it resembles ground pork, then wrap it in a towel and squeeze out the water. Turn into a bowl and toss with the chipotle powder and mushroom soy sauce.

2. Puree half the vinegar with the garlic, oregano, cumin, and coriander seeds. Add the chile and blend until smooth, then add the remaining vinegar along with the chard, cilantro, and parsley. Blend until you have a bright green puree.

3. Combine the puree with the tofu, bread crumbs, salt, and eggs, if using. Toss well. Before cooking the entire mixture, check the seasoning by frying a little of it, then tasting it. I find that with the vinegar and chile, this is enough salt, if not add more, then heat the oil in a wide skillet and fry until golden.

Green "Chorizo"

MAKES ABOUT 4 CUPS

Based on a Mexican recipe for green chorizo which uses chard and herbs, these "sausage" crumbles leave your lips and mouth on fire. While here tofu takes the place of pork, you could use a mixture of part tofu and part pork for flavor. The finished mixture made without the eggs is cooked, crumbled, then added to scrambled eggs, used in quesadillas, or with home fries. If you add the eggs, the mixture will hold its shape and the "sausage" can be formed into little patties.

Spicy Red "Sausage"

MAKES ABOUT 1 1/2 CUPS

*The seasonings here are based
on the more frequently seen
red chorizo.*

1 carton extra-firm or firm tofu

1/3 cup mild vinegar, apple cider,
  or white wine vinegar

1 tablespoon canola oil

4 plump garlic cloves

1/2 teaspoon dried thyme

1 bay leaf

1 teaspoon ground cumin

1/2 teaspoon ground allspice

1/4 teaspoon black pepper

1/8 teaspoon ground cloves

1/2 teaspoon salt

1/2 teaspoon ground chipotle chile
  (optional)

1 tablespoon mild ground red chile

1 tablespoon paprika

1/2 cup chopped cilantro

Vegetable oil

1. Crumble the tofu, wrap it in a dish towel, squeeze out the water, then turn it into a bowl.

2. Combine the vinegar with the remaining ingredients in a small food processor or blender. Puree until smooth, then pour over the tofu and toss well. Taste for salt and pepper.

3. To cook, heat 1 tablespoon vegetable oil in a skillet, add the mixture, and cook over medium-high heat until it's fairly dry and crumbly, but still tender. At this point you can stir it into scrambled eggs, add it to a breakfast burrito, or home-fried potatoes, and so forth.

2 teaspoons vegetable oil

1 cup Spicy Red "Sausage" (page 106)

3 eggs (or 5 egg whites), lightly beaten

2 tablespoons chopped cilantro

1 scallion, including the tiny green, chopped

Salt

¼ cup grated Muenster, Jack, or smoked Cheddar cheese

2 wheat tortillas

Salsa or hot sauce

Scrambled Eggs with Spicy Red "Sausage" in Tortillas

SERVES 2

1. Heat the oil in a medium nonstick skillet. When hot, add the "sausage" and cook over medium-high heat, turning frequently, until heated through and browning in places.

2. Add the cilantro, scallion, and a few pinches of salt to the eggs. Pour them into the pan, add the cheese, and cook, stirring slowly but continually, until the eggs are set.

3. Meanwhile, warm the tortillas in a second skillet or on an *asador,* a stove top grill that sits over the burner. Turn them so that both sides are hot. Wrap the scrambled eggs in the tortillas, and serve with salsa.

Migas

Eggs (and tofu, too) scrambled with crunchy tortilla chips are good for any meal. You can make your own chips or—just as good and, frankly, more convenient—use tortilla chips straight from the bag. Serve with warm wheat or corn tortillas and salsa.

½ carton soft tofu

1½ tablespoons olive oil or butter or a mixture of oil and butter

2 pinches turmeric

1 jalapeño chile, seeded and diced

3 scallions, slit lengthwise, then chopped

Salt

2 eggs, lightly beaten, or 1 egg and 2 egg whites

¼ cup chopped cilantro

2 Roma tomatoes, seeded and chopped

½ cup grated Muenster or Monterey Jack cheese

2 heaping cups of tortilla chips (See Note)

1. Press the tofu (page 7) to get most of the water out while you gather the rest of your ingredients.

2. Heat a medium nonstick skillet and add the oil. When hot, crumble the tofu into the pan into pieces about the size of scrambled-egg curds. Sprinkle with the turmeric, add the chile and scallions, and season with ½ teaspoon salt. Cook over high heat, stirring occasionally, until any water remaining in the tofu has cooked away, but not so long that the tofu turns hard. It should remain a little tender, like scrambled eggs.

3. Pour in the eggs and add the cilantro and tomatoes. Reduce the heat a little and cook, stirring constantly, until the eggs are nearly as dry as you like them. Add the cheese and tortilla chips and continue cooking until the eggs are done. Serve onto plates with a slotted spoon so that any remaining water from the tofu stays in the pan.

All Tofu Migas: If you're not using eggs, use the entire carton of tofu and an extra pinch of turmeric to give them a nice yellow hue. Once the tofu has firmed up, add the cilantro, tomatoes, cheese, and tortillas, cook until the cheese is melted and everything is hot.

Note: To make your own corn chips, start with corn tortillas—stale, if possible—and cut them into strips or wedges. Spray lightly with oil or leave dry. Bake at 425°F until crisp or microwave a single layer of chips at a time, for 1 minute on high, then turn and microwave for 40 seconds longer, or until crisp.

Scrambled Tofu with Herbs and Cheese

SERVES 3 TO 4

1 carton soft tofu

1 tablespoon olive oil

2 teaspoons butter

¼ teaspoon turmeric or curry powder

Salt and freshly ground black pepper

2 tablespoons chopped parsley

2 tablespoons chopped tarragon, basil, or marjoram

2 tablespoons snipped chives or finely sliced scallions

½ cup grated Cheddar, Muenster, goat, or feta cheese

Paprika

1. Drain the tofu, wrap it in a towel, and press while you gather the rest of the ingredients.

2. Heat the oil and butter in a medium skillet. When hot, crumble the tofu into the pan in pieces about the size of scrambled-egg curds. Sprinkle with the turmeric, season with ½ teaspoon salt, and cook over medium-high heat, stirring frequently, until dry and firm (but not hard), for 3 to 5 minutes.

3. Add the herbs and cheese, taste and season with salt, then season with pepper. Serve with a dash of paprika over the top.

1 carton soft tofu

1¹/₂ tablespoons safflower or canola oil

3 tablespoons finely diced onion

1 serrano or 1 jalapeño chile, seeded and diced

¹/₂ teaspoon ground cumin

¹/₄ teaspoon dried oregano

¹/₄ teaspoon ground chipotle powder, or more to taste (optional)

¹/₈ teaspoon turmeric or curry powder

3 tablespoons chopped cilantro

Salt

¹/₂ cup grated smoked Cheddar or smoked Mozzarella cheese

Salsa

Smoky Scrambled Tofu with Tomatoes and Chile

SERVES 3

You can also add eggs to the pan once the tofu is cooked. Serve in corn or wheat tortillas with your favorite salsa.

1. Drain the tofu, wrap it in a towel, and press while you gather the rest of your ingredients.

2. Heat the oil in a skillet, add the onion and sauté over high heat for 1 or 2 minutes to sear. Add the chile, cumin, oregano, and ground chipotle, and cook for 1 or 2 minutes more.

3. Crumble the tofu into the pan, sprinkle over the turmeric, and cook, stirring frequently, until dry and firm. Season with ¹/₂ teaspoon salt and stir in the cilantro and cheese. Serve with warm tortillas and salsa.

SMOOTHIES AND THEIR COUSINS, good at any time, tend to serve as a substitute for the sit-down, solid breakfast. Fortunately, one can find portable sustenance along with good flavor in a smoothie.

While I've long been comfortable sipping a smoothie made with soy milk, the idea of drinking pureed tofu did make me nervous. Once I gave it a try, I had to admit that it was pretty good. Good enough that I'm confident that even the most reluctant among us will be pleasantly surprised. Tofu works especially well in drinks that you want to be smooth and creamy (but not made that way with banana), such as those based on coffee or juice. Tofu, however, does have a presence, so strong surrounding flavors are recommended. For this reason you may have better success if you base your smoothies on soy milk, and use tofu in small quantities as a thickener. Silken tofu purees most nicely, but you can use any type except extra-firm regular tofu. One-half to 1 cup are ample for 2 servings.

Don't take the measurements given here too seriously. They're just to get you started. After you've made one or two smoothies you'll be concocting your own combinations with flair. You'll also develop a keen eye for things that used to be bothersome, like a half-pot of espresso that's gone cold, a little coconut milk begging to be used, a dollop of peanut butter, the tail end of some lemon curd, or a pear that's grown a little too soft to serve. All of these can be easily turned into delicious beverages.

The ice cubes, by the way, are for making your smoothie cold. Leave them out, if you really don't care, or briefly freeze the fresh fruit and skip the ice. If you like protein powders and the like, go ahead and add them to your drinks as well.

1/2 box silken tofu (soft or firm both work)

1 cup sliced strawberries

2 medium bananas

1 cup milk (skim, soy milk, or if you're a fan, buttermilk)

1 teaspoon honey or maple syrup

1/2 cup ice cubes

In a food processor or blender, puree the tofu and fruit until smooth, gradually adding the milk to loosen the mixture. Add the honey and ice and continue to blend until smooth.

1/4 pound silken tofu

2 large, juicy ripe peaches or nectarines

1/2 teaspoon vanilla

2 drops almond extract

1 teaspoon light honey or maple syrup, to taste

1 cup soy milk or buttermilk

1/2 cup ice

Put the tofu and peaches in the blender with the vanilla and almond extracts and puree until smooth. Add the honey, milk, and ice, continue to blend until smooth, then serve.

Mark's Tofu Shake

SERVES 4

Chef Mark Mattern of Disney World shared his recipe with me for a tofu shake he serves to guests to break the ice before the start of their Healthy Cooking Program. He said that they have absolutely no idea the beverage they were enjoying so much was based on tofu. Such was his success that he uses this recipe at home on his unsuspecting children—with equal success.

Peach-Almond Smoothie

SERVES 4

A drop or two of almond extract tastes good with all stone fruits, such as peaches, nectarines, plums, cherries, and apricots. Try any of these fruits, alone or together, to make this smoothie.

Fruits and Flavorings for Smoothies

Many fruits and flavorings keep good company with tofu and soy milk.

FRUITS

guavas

pineapples

plums

apricots

cherries (pitted, of course)

mangoes

papayas

peaches and nectarines

seedless muscat grapes

ripe pears

berries of all kinds

melons

dates

kiwi fruit

JUICES

apple

white grape

cranberry

fruit nectars, such as guava and apricot

coconut and coconut pineapple

mango and papaya

FLAVORINGS AND ADDITIONS

vanilla

almond extract

fresh lime juice

fresh lemon juice

fresh mint or lemon verbena

syrups, such as almond, hazelnut, cassis, and others

strong coffee or espresso

cinnamon

nutmeg

chocolate

nut butters

OTHER INGREDIENTS

yogurt

sherbets

ice cream

rice and almond drinks

½ cup silken tofu

1 large, ripe banana

1 to 1½ cups soy milk

1 teaspoon vanilla

½ teaspoon orange flower water (optional)

1 teaspoon light honey, to taste

freshly grated nutmeg

5 ice cubes

In the blender puree the tofu with the banana until smooth, then gradually add the milk and flavorings. Add the ice and puree again until smooth. Pour into glasses and scrape a little nutmeg over the top.

Variations: ¼ cup peanut butter or almond butter • 2 tablespoons or more chocolate syrup • both peanut butter and chocolate syrup • ½ cup coconut milk plus a squeeze of fresh lime

The All-Banana Shake

SERVES 2

Personally, I've always liked a banana smoothie that's pure bananas, especially when it has lots of vanilla in it. This comes from enjoying a few liquados *one winter in Mexico, which tasted of bananas, vanilla, and thick Mexican cream. It was like sipping melted ice cream through a straw. But back to tofu . . .*

Date Shakes

Date shakes are one of the perennial treats found at date gardens in California's Coachella Valley. Made with ice cream and dates, they are very sweet and rich. Using yogurt and/or tofu in place of some or all of the ice cream makes them a little less intense and allows more of the delicious date flavor to come forward. If you're using dates that have hardened, steam them over boiling water or in the microwave until they're soft, so that they can be successfully pureed.

½ cup soft dates, preferably Medjools or Deglet Noors

1 cup soy milk

5 ice cubes

½ cup yogurt, ice cream, or silken tofu

½ teaspoon vanilla

½ teaspoon orange flower water

Put the dates and soy milk in a blender and blend on low speed until the dates are completely broken up. This can take a few minutes. Add the remaining ingredients and blend at high speed until smooth and cold. Serve in small glasses.

½ box silken tofu

2 cups guava nectar

Juice of 1 lime

1 small mango or 1 cup frozen raspberries

5 ice cubes

Passion fruit syrup (optional)

Combine the first four ingredients in the blender and puree until smooth. Stir in the passion fruit syrup, if desired, to taste.

Tropical Smoothie

SERVES 3

Fresh guavas would be ideal, but not many of us have them growing in our backyards. Guava nectar, available in cans or aseptic packages, has plenty of that lovely tropical flavor, and a few spoonfuls of passion fruit syrup (or one fresh passion fruit) will complete the island effect. Garnish the drink with, if not a passion fruit flower, then maybe a sprig of honey-suckle.

1 ripe, juicy mango

2 teaspoons light brown sugar

½ cup coconut milk or ½ cup
   pineapple-coconut nectar

1 cup soy milk

Juice of 1 or 2 limes, to taste

5 ice cubes

Mint or jasmine sprigs, for garnish

Peel the mango, then slice it right over the blender jar to catch all the juices. Once you've cut off the big chunks of mango, just squeeze your hand over the whole thing to get off as much flesh and juice as possible. Add all the other ingredients to the blender and puree until smooth. Pour into 2 glasses and garnish with mint.

Mango Smoothie

SERVES 2

This thick and silky drink has the prettiest color and the loveliest perfume. Make it often in early summer when mangoes are plentiful.

Peanut Butter Smoothie

SERVES 4

This drink made me rediscover peanut butter, of all things. Add a tablespoon or two of chocolate syrup, and you're close to imbibing a liquid peanut butter cup. A small cup of brewed espresso or other strong coffee also goes great with peanut butter.

1¹/₂ cups soy milk
¹/₂ cup silken tofu
¹/₃ cup peanut butter
1 tablespoon honey
1 banana
5 ice cubes

Puree the soy milk and tofu in the blender until smooth, scraping down the sides once or twice. Add the remaining ingredients and puree once more until smooth and cold. Serve in small glasses.

Iced Coffee Frappe

SERVES 2

Once you start making smooth-ies with espresso you'll plan to have leftover coffee. You can vary these endlessly, with the additions suggested, but here's one that's more or less pure iced coffee and not too thick.

1 cup cold strong coffee or espresso
¹/₂ cup soy milk
¹/₃ cup soft silken tofu
3 ice cubes
1 teaspoon vanilla
1 tablespoon brown sugar

Combine everything in the blender and puree until smooth.

Variations: pinch cinnamon or nutmeg • vanilla • hazelnut or almond syrup • chocolate syrup • coconut milk • a big scoop of vanilla ice cream or frozen yogurt • a banana

MOST OF THE TOFU DISHES IN THIS BOOK are brightly seasoned with spicy, pungent, hot, sour, sweet, and salty ingredients—ginger and chile, soy sauce, tamarind, garlic, rice wine, and of course, curry spices. Consequently, they tend to go best with foods that are rather neutral, and what could be more perfect than rice, the ideal foil for such complex lively seasonings? Rice is nice, but change is always welcome on occasion, and that's when I turn to sweet potatoes as an alternative accompaniment, their sweetness being friendly to the ginger-soy-chile triad. Here are some basic recipes for both rice and sweet potatoes so that you can round out your tofu dishes.

Rice

You may already have your own perfect way of cooking rice. However, there's more than one way, and it partly depends on the rice you use, long- or short-grain, white or brown.

Long-Grain
White Rice I

SERVES 4

1¹/₂ cups long-grain rice

2¹/₄ cups water

¹/₄ teaspoon salt

1.   Combine the rice, water, and salt in a medium, heavy saucepan with a tight-fitting lid.

2.   Bring to a boil, then reduce the heat to low and cover the pot. Cook until the water has been absorbed and the rice is tender, 15 to 18 minutes. If it's not quite done but the pot seems dry, add a few tablespoons water, re-cover, and let steam for 5 more minutes. Gently separate the grains with a fork before serving. ●

Long-Grain
White Rice II

SERVES 4

Because the amount of water is determined by how deeply it covers the rice, you can make this in any quantity by eye. This is the method I use most commonly at home. To end up with perfectly cooked rice, use the same pot each time you make it so that you can develop your eye for the proper water level, and a good sense of timing.

1¹/₂ cups long-grain rice

¹/₄ teaspoon salt

Put the rice and salt in a medium, heavy saucepan and add water to cover by 1 inch (about 3 cups.) Bring to a boil, then continue boiling over medium heat until most of the liquid on the surface has evaporated or been absorbed and the surface looks as if it's covered with little craters. This should take 15 to 18 minutes. Now reduce the heat as low as it will go and cover the pan with a tight-fitting lid. Cook for 15 minutes, or until tender. ●

1½ cups basmati rice

2¼ cups water

1 teaspoon ghee, butter, or oil (optional)

¼ teaspoon salt

1.   Rinse the rice in several changes of water, then drain and put in a medium, heavy saucepan. Add the water and let soak for 20 minutes.

2.   Bring to a boil, add the ghee, if using, and salt, then reduce the heat to low. Cover and cook until the rice is tender, about 12 minutes. Turn off the heat and let stand until all the water is absorbed and the rice is fluffy, about 5 minutes. Fluff the grains with a fork before serving.

You can cook basmati, a long-grain rice, using either of the preceding methods, or you can make it according to a more traditional, Indian method, which involves soaking the rice first so that the grains can expand.

Brown Rice: The amount of water and cooking time for brown rice vary, depending on how the rice is processed and whether it's short- or long-grain rice. It also shortens the cooking time some if you can soak the rice first for an hour. If you buy it in a package, check the instructions. If you buy it in bulk, my general rule of thumb is:

For 1 cup long-grain brown rice, use 2⅛ cups water

For 1 cup short-grain brown rice, use 2¼ cups water

Combine rice and water in a saucepan, add a pinch of salt, and bring to a boil. Lower the heat and cover tightly. Cook for 45 minutes without disturbing. Taste the rice. If it's still a little too firm but the water has been absorbed, spoon several tablespoons of water over the surface, return the lid, and continue cooking until the rice is done. Repeat if necessary.

Sweet Potatoes

Sweet potatoes go well with those tofu dishes that are full of ginger and soy, and they make a nice change from rice and noodles as accompaniments. Choose organic sweet potatoes and you can enjoy eating the skins; just give them a good scrubbing first. Don't, by the way, bypass the delicious Garnet and Jewel yams. They are, in fact, sweet potatoes. Here are various ways to prepare them.

Steamed Sweet Potatoes: Allow one medium (8- to 10-ounce) tuber per person. Scrub well, then place on a steaming rack over boiling water and cook, covered, for about 30 minutes. Pierce them with a knife to check for doneness. The knife should just slide in.

Pressure Cooked Sweet Potatoes: Place scrubbed sweet potatoes in the pressure cooker on a rack over water. Secure the lid, bring to pressure, then cook on high for 15 minutes. Quickly release the pressure, open the lid, and check for doneness. If they're not quite cooked, return the lid and simply steam until done. It should only be a matter of minutes.

The pressure cooker is a great tool to use when you intend to make a puree of your sweet potatoes, as it cooks them to such tenderness and so quickly.

Sweet Potato Puree: Cook sweet potatoes until they're absolutely tender, then mash them with a fork, including the skin, if you wish. Season with salt and pepper, a little butter if you like, or dark sesame oil.

2 pounds sweet potatoes, peeled or scrubbed

$1/2$ cup orange juice

2 teaspoons canola oil

Plenty of freshly ground black pepper

$1/8$ teaspoon ground red chile

$1/2$ teaspoon salt

1. Preheat the oven to 400°F.

2. Quarter the sweet potatoes lengthwise, then cut them crosswise into chunks about $1/2$ inch or more across.

3. Put the sweet potatoes in a large baking dish, add the remaining ingredients, and toss well.

4. Cover with aluminum foil and bake for 40 minutes. Remove the foil, give the potatoes a stir, and continue baking until tender and glazed, another 20 minutes or so.

Sweet Potatoes Baked with Orange

SERVES 4

These are especially well suited to accompany very simple tofu dishes.

Asian Vegetarian Feast. Ken Hom. New York: William Morrow & Company, 1988.

The Bold Vegetarian. Bharti Kirchner. New York: HarperCollins, 1995.

The Bombay Cafe. Neela Paniz. Berkeley: Ten Speed Press, 1998.

The Book of Tofu. William Shurtleff & Akiko Aoyagi. Berkeley: Ten Speed Press, 1975.

Bruce Cost's Asian Ingredients. New York: William Morrow & Company, 1988.

Cafespice Namaste. Cyrus Todiwala. San Francisco: Soma Books, 1998.

From the Earth, Chinese Vegetarian Cooking. Eileen Yin-Fei Lo. New York: Macmillan, 1995.

Indian Grill: The Art of Tandoori Cooking at Home. Smita Chardia. New Jersey: The Ecco Press, 1999.

Lee Wade's Korean Cookery. Edited by Joan Rutt and Sandra Mattielli. New Jersey: Hollym, 1985.

The Natural Kitchen: Soy! Dana Jacobi. Rockland, CA: Prima Publishing, 1996.

The New Soy Cookbook. Lorna Sass. San Francisco: Chronicle Books, 1998.

Real Vegetarian Thai. Nancie McDermott. San Francisco: Chronicle Books, 1997.

Vatch's Southeast Asian Cookbook. Vatcharin Bumichitir. New York: St. Martin's Press, 1997.

World-of-the-East, Madhur Jaffrey's Vegetarian Cooking. New York: Alfred A. Knopf, 1981.

Index